Stepping Out of the BOAT

McDougal & Associates
Servants of Christ and Stewards of the Mysteries of God

Stepping Out of the BOAT

A STUDY ON FAITH

BY
CRYSTAL CALLAIS

Published by:

McDougal & Associates
18896 Greenwell Springs RD
Greenwell Springs, LA 70739
www.thepublishedword.com

McDougal & Associates is dedicated to spreading the Gospel
of the Lord Jesus Christ to as many people as possible
in the shortest time possible.

ISBN 978-1-950398-37-9

Printed in the U.S., the U.K. and Australia
For Worldwide Distribution

DEDICATION

This book is dedicated to you, readers who are ready to step out of your comfort zone. Maybe you feel that God is calling you into a new ministry, a new job, or into a new season of your life. Stepping into the unknown can be scary and intimidating. There are so many distractions that arise, wanting to pull our eyes off of Jesus. My prayer for you is that, as you read the following pages, the Holy Spirit will grow your faith in mighty ways. I know you will be strengthened in areas needed for your journey. Keep your eyes on Jesus as you step out of your comfort zone, even into the storm that may arise around you.

ACKNOWLEDGMENTS

I would like to, first, give thanks to God, my Heavenly Father, for the revelations and the strength I found in my quiet time with Him. As I was spending time daily in His presence, the journey He has brought me through has grown my faith in a way that allowed me to step out of my comfort zone in one area I had been trapped in, also in areas that I was unaware of. The Holy Spirit then led me through the Scriptures in a way that has strengthened my faith like never before. My heart yearns that, as you read through the following pages and study the scripture passages that follow, the LORD God will bring you on your journey with Him in a way that will grow and strengthen your faith in Him as well.

I would also like to acknowledge those who helped me with encouragement, editing and development of this book:

- **Russell Callais, my forever friend and husband.** Thank you for believing in me and encouraging me to keep writing. You are a strength when I need it. Thank you for encouraging me to step out of my comfort zone in crazy, amazing ways when the LORD God asked me to. Watching your walk with the LORD God is a true inspiration. I love you!

- **Lorraine Foret, my mom, and Kayla Voisin, my sister.** Thank you for the countless hours you spent in the reading and proofing of this book. Thank you for believing in me and helping me when times were rough and feelings to quit arose. You are both a vital part of my life. I love you both.
- **Kim and Vanessa Voisin, my pastors.** Thank you for being who God called you to be. I've watched you both be obedient when God speaks to you to do or say something. You have both encouraged me to be obedient in the small things which lead to the bigger things. Your excitement for what God is doing in Russell's and my life is genuine and encouraging. Thank you for both supporting us to reach for the stars.
- **Joshua Mills.** Thank you for your endorsement as well as for being obedient to the LORD God when you visited our church. You gave a prophetic word saying that the LORD was releasing, to anyone who wanted it, "revelatory knowledge and the ability to write the revelations in a way that others can understand it." I raised my hand and told the LORD I wanted that knowledge and ability, and that I was a willing vessel for Him to use. Things have been turning in my spirit man ever since.
- **Mr. Harold.** Thank you for your patience and guidance as we worked through the editing of this book. Your insight has been appreciated.
- **Friends and family.** Thank you for your encouragement to keep writing. You inspire me to keep pressing into God.

CONTENTS

It's time to step out of your comfort zone and encounter Jesus in a new and amazing way.

— **Crystal**

FOREWORD BY REV. KIM VOISIN

In this compilation of faith events and stories, Crystal Callais' writings are informative, inspiring and challenging. She is extremely sound and invites her reader's attention to some prominent aspects of faith. The journey through many faith-building events will draw your desires to take a leap of faith in your own life. Consuming the pages of Crystal's writings will help build a foundation for a dynamic Christian life. Be prepared to be challenged and equipped to step out of your comfort zone.

Rev. Kim F. Voisin, PhD.
Pastor, Vision Christian Center
Bourg, Louisiana

FOREWORD BY J.D. SMITH

Staying in the boat of their comfort zone allows most people to coast through life, while stepping out of your comfort zone allows for extraordinary encounters you wouldn't otherwise experience. Amazing rewards are available for you as you allow the Holy Spirit to stretch and mature your faith in all areas, even the areas you may be unaware need stretching.

Take this journey with Crystal Callais, as she strategically brings you through God's Holy Word in a way that you will see more of God's greatness and unlock your potential to step out of your comfort zone and walk on the water with Jesus, as Peter did.

Get copies for yourself, your family, your friends and even your enemies, as you step out and step into the new that God has for you!

J.D. Smith
Pastor/Founder CitiImpact Ministries
Founder, JDSmithOnline.com

FOREWORD BY JOSHUA MILLS

Faith … It seems like such a simple subject and many talk about it, but when it comes right down to living it, actually getting out of the boat and facing the raging winds and waves, many falter. Peter did too. I'm sure we have all faced some storms that seemed to threaten our wellbeing and have left us frightened and discouraged, sinking in doubt and despair. I know I have.

The wonderful thing is that Peter's story has a happy ending. He realized that he needed to get his focus off of those winds and waves and back onto Jesus, he cried out to the Lord for help, and he was lifted up out of the water's grasp. He was then able to walk victoriously with Jesus on the waves of the sea. Faith becomes a miraculous force when it is focused on Christ!

For several years now, I have had the privilege of ministering periodically at Vision Christian Center in Bourg, Louisiana, and have come to think of its leaders and members as family. And they are, part of this big family of God. Crystal Callais and her husband, Rusty, are part of that body, and it has been my joy to see them growing and expanding in their personal life of faith each time I have visited.

In recent months, Crystal has taken some big steps of faith, one of them the writing of this book. In it, she bares her soul and transparently allows us to follow her own personal journey, with its ups and downs, victories and defeats, as she has moved ever higher in her relationship with the Lord and her understanding and daily operation of what it means to have faith in God.

That faith, she shows us, affects every part of our daily life — how we think, what we say, how we act and react. If we take the right steps, our faith grows ... until suddenly we realize that everything is now possible to us through Jesus Christ. As you read this book, I believe the Spirit will give you greater faith for the greater glory.

I encourage every reader to take this journey with Crystal, that you may one day hear the Lord's voice welcoming you, saying, *"Well done, good and faithful servant. Enter into the joy of the Lord."* It's time to begin *Stepping Out of the Boat*.

Joshua Mills

INTRODUCTION

This study on faith was inspired when I was personally seeking God to build my own faith big enough to feel as though I was ready to take the first step out of the boat of my comfort zone. The Holy Spirit had already spoken to me about writing a devotional, which I did. Then the LORD my God said, "I want you to step out and give it [the devotional] to several people within your home church that you admire very highly to be critiqued." That was a difficult moment for me. God was telling me, "Get out of the boat of your comfort zone and follow Me."

I wasn't sure how to build myself up to be brave enough to do what the Lord was asking of me. I instantly thought of all the negative possibilities that could happen as I would take this step of faith. I started to seek God, studying to build my own faith. As I dove into the Word, the Holy Spirit started to reveal to me areas that I needed to allow Him to heal. The wounds in those areas were hindering me from fully trusting Him and stepping out in blind faith. Rejection, betrayal and being gossiped about were some of the things I had to let go of on a deeper level than I had before so that I could fully trust the LORD my God as I began to take this step of faith that He was asking of me.

The Lord began to show me the way I viewed other people, and that the outcomes of those situations were ultimately the same lenses I viewed Him through. As I began to heal and began stepping out of the boat of my comfort zone, I saw God opening amazing doors in my life and the life of my family members. God aligned every step He wanted me to take before I even knew I needed that step.

As time progressed, God opened other doors in other parts of our ministry which He was asking me to walk through as well. In stepping out of the boat of my comfort zone, I have had to make myself vulnerable before the LORD and also before other people on a deeper level than I was accustomed to. This was difficult at the beginning because I wasn't aware of just how small my faith was in that one area of my life. I hadn't realized that the walls of self-protection I had put up were hindering my relationship with the LORD my God.

What you will see on the following pages are the passages of scripture the LORD used to heal me and grow my faith. And it worked. My faith is bigger today than it was yesterday. The LORD God has now asked me to share my heart with you. This study will parallel with passages in your own Bible. I will present a variety of summaries and/or examples followed by questions the Holy Spirit asked me as I studied these passages myself. I believe He will use this study to heal your heart, as He did mine, in areas you know it needs healing, as well as areas of wounding you may not be aware of.

This study is designed in a way that you can do a small group study, with several people diving in and discussing the scripture passages, or you may choose to do an in-depth study on your own. The choice is yours!

My desire for you is that your faith will grow deeper as you begin stepping out of the boat of your comfort zone. As you step out of the boat, you will see the LORD moving in a mighty way, aligning your steps one in front the other and leading you to greater victories. It's time to step out of your comfort zone and encounter Jesus in a new and amazing way.

Crystal Callais
Houma, Louisiana

CHAPTER 1

TAKING A STEP OF FAITH

Matthew 14:22-33

Immediately following the miraculous feeding of five thousand people with two loaves and five fish, Jesus then sent His disciples on a boat to the other side of the Sea of Galilee. While they were being obedient in crossing the sea, Jesus sent the multitudes away and went to a mountain to pray alone. When the disciples were in the boat in the midst of the sea, a sudden storm came up. The waves grew strong and began to beat against the sides of the boat.

Think about your life right now and what your boat may consist of. Maybe all is going well for you. Maybe you just watched Jesus move in a miraculous way in your life or in someone else's life around you, similar to the disciples watching Jesus feed five thousand men (not counting women and children). Maybe Jesus has done a miracle in front of you today or has even worked through you to perform a miracle. Now, He is telling you what step He wants you to take next.

Maybe this is your next assignment or the next season in your life or ministry. He may speak to you through a nudge in your spirit or by prophecy spoken over you by someone else. For the first-century disciples, the first step in their next assignment from Jesus was to get in the boat and head across the Sea of Galilee.

What is my calling or next assignment?

_____

_____

_____

What step is Jesus asking me to take?

_____

_____

_____

Am I submissive to His voice? If not, what thoughts am I submissive to?

_____

_____

_____

Think about this: when you are in rough waters in a boat, how do you feel? Frightened or nervous? You may have a ton of thoughts of the possible negative situations that could arise. Think about the disciples. They could have questioned in their minds why Jesus would even send them out in a boat if He knew a storm would arise.

Once I submit and I'm following His direction, have I ever found myself second-guessing why Jesus would ask this of me?

_____

_____

_____

Do I trust in His protection? If not, where have I misplaced my trust?

_____

_____

_____

Am I feeling doubt or perhaps second-guessing whether I heard Jesus tell me to get in the boat in the first place?

_____

_____

_____

Am I nervous?

_____

_____

_____

You know Jesus told you to do something, but in the process of being submissive, you are starting to wonder and fear the unknown. (For example, you may be hearing thoughts of "What if I fail?") As you are submissively doing what Jesus is asking of you, you are taking that initial step of faith. Then, as soon as you step out in faith, your reality stirs up your emotions, and you feel a storm coming. You are still safe, but you feel the wind and waves of your emotions, and all sorts of thoughts come crashing in around you.

What emotions do I currently feel?

_____

_____

_____

What thoughts am I hearing in my head or from others that are fueling these emotions?

_____

_____

_____

Between three and six in the morning, Jesus came walking on the water toward the disciples. Now, remember: the disciples had been in that boat, being beaten by the wind and waves all night long. They were probably physically and emotionally exhausted. Think of a time where the circumstances of your reality felt like they were crashing in around you, one after another. When you are tired, weary and overwhelmed, you start to see things happening in your reality that you may or may not even understand.

What things are happening in my life in this moment that I may not understand?

_____

_____

_____

And when the disciples saw him walking on the sea, they were troubled, saying, It is a spirit; and they cried out for fear.

Matthew 14:26

There is a difference between being troubled and being fearful. *Troubled* means "to stir or agitate"[1] while *fear* refers to "alarm or fright."[2] The disciples didn't know what they were seeing. If they had known who it was or possibly felt that they had control, they wouldn't have been troubled by their stirring emotions. But, because their emotions were stirring, and they didn't understand what their eyes were seeing, fear gripped them.

What area or areas do I see that cause me to be troubled?

_____

_____

_____

How do I counteract that fear?

_____

_____

_____

The disciples faced the fear together. They had each other. They possibly reasoned out in their minds: if someone was walking on the water, it must be a ghost. Immediately Jesus comforted them, addressing their fear:

1. He went against their fear by saying, *"Take courage"* (Matthew 14:27, AMP).
2. He went against their lack of understanding by saying, *"It is I"* (Matthew 14:27, AMP).

1. *Strong's* —G#5015
2. *Strong's*—G#5401

There are times when we don't see God in our reality simply because we don't understand what is happening. He may be showing up in a way we are unfamiliar with. When we are being hit by and beat up by the wind and waves of our reality and feel exhausted, it is time to look away from the boat and look to Jesus. Jesus is there! He is always there.

Where is Jesus in my situation?
Where is my focus?

_____

_____

_____

Once Peter realized that it was Jesus, he responded, wanting permission to get out of the boat. Jesus said to him, *"Come"* (Matthew 14:29). Peter responded to what Jesus had said, and what an amazing opportunity Peter had! Peter got out of the boat to meet Jesus on the water.

Do I seek the Lord for permission, waiting for Him to tell me, "It is time," or do I act in my own timing?

_____

_____

_____

What step of faith am I currently taking or trying to take in order to step out of the boat of my comfort zone?

_____

_____

_____

Peter wasn't worried about exposing his weakness. His focus was on Jesus and not on the other disciples with him.

How often do you say, "God use me. I am a willing vessel?" I have said it before out of the excitement of the moment, and many people I know have said the same thing. I know that personally my gift mix is in being a teacher. I have taught small groups, Sunday school, youth group and more. Still, when God said, "I'll use you as a vessel. I want you to teach others how to heal the way I taught you," I froze. In my heart I thought of every reason why I shouldn't and couldn't do what He was asking of me. I told God things like: "People will talk about me," "They will judge me," "They will think I'm crazy," or "They don't want to hear what I have to say." God was saying to me, "Come," and I was answering, "No, I can't. I will fail because I'm not good enough."

The key is that Peter couldn't walk on the water in his own ability. He was only able to walk on the water in God's ability.

What can I do to keep my focus on Jesus instead of the storm? (See Philippians 4:6-9.)

_____

_____

_____

Do I guard myself from the negativity of others and try to do things on my own, so that others don't see my vulnerability?

_____

_____

_____

**What accountability or guardrails can I set up
to keep me going in the right direction?**

_____

_____

_____

A Challenge: Find additional scripture references
            to stand on that will maintain you
            firmly rooted and write them below.

But when he saw [the effects of] the wind, he was frightened, and he began to sink, and he cried out, "Lord, save me!"

Matthew 14:30, AMP

According to the Scriptures, Peter saw the wind, felt fear, and then started to sink. The first thing Peter did was to take his eyes off of Jesus and focus on what the wind was doing.

It is easy to ask Jesus for direction or ask Him to open a door. When He does, it is sometimes easy to take the first step of faith out of the boat and be obedient to the Lord. At other times, however, it is not all that easy. Regardless, Peter was able to do it ... UNTIL he started focusing on the wind, which was his reality.

Reality will always do something to try and distract you. You will see the effects of the wind all around you. People may say negative things, things that you expect may or may not happen, and disappointments may arise. But your reality does NOT need to affect or influence your decision to step out in faith. When you take your eyes off of Jesus and focus on reality, you will start to sink, just as Peter did.

Am I focused on Jesus and walking out in obedience to Him?

_____

_____

_____

If so, what change is Jesus doing through me that others can see?

_____

_____

_____

Am I focused on the wind, and because of it, sinking and screaming for Jesus to move in and save me?

_____

_____

_____

If so, what wind am I focused on, and how do I get my eyes back on Jesus?

_____

_____

_____

What would block me from placing my focus back on the Lord?

_____

_____

_____

Things that could possibly be blocking you are offenses, which are perceptions, assumptions or expectations. You could be in unforgiveness, bitterness, resentment or envy, etc.

If I choose not to step out of the boat, what regrets would I have to live with?

_____

_____

_____

Think for a moment about the other disciples in the boat with Peter in that moment. They chose to stay in the boat rather than ask and step out in faith the way Peter did. Think about what Peter could have faced, just from within the boat, from his companions. He could have been influenced by their encouragement to step out of the boat or their discouragement not to step out the boat. He would have had to choose whether or not to put what others were saying over what Jesus was telling him. Thankfully, Peter didn't allow anything other than the words of Jesus to affect his decision to step out of the boat.

There are people in the boat with you right now as well. They are your inner circle of friends and family, the people you surround yourself with. They could be a positive influence or a negative influence on the decisions you make in your everyday life in your walk with Jesus. Do they encourage you to stretch your faith and believe God that you can do the impossible? Or do they encourage you to stay in the safety of the boat?

Do the fears, dangers, or expectations of others hold me back?

_____

_____

_____

Notice that when Peter started to walk on the water, it was easier for him to exercise faith in that moment because he had his eyes on Jesus. The passage goes on to describe the status of Peter's faith moments later:

And immediately Jesus stretched forth his hand, and caught him, and said unto him, O thou of little faith, wherefore didst thou doubt? Matthew 14:31

Notice: when Jesus told Peter to come, Peter responded with obedience. When Peter's focus shifted from Jesus to the wind, something happened to his faith.

According to Hebrews 11, faith is what we cannot see. When Peter's focus shifted to what reality around him was saying, could it be that he was no longer operating with faith and obedience, but now actually operating in limited faith and doubt?

When Peter started to sink, he called out to Jesus. In response to Peter's plea, Jesus stretched out His hand to save him. Jesus didn't just speak to Peter; there was an immediate action that Peter could see. Peter had to choose to accept the hand and trust that this hand would help him. And, of course, it did.

There will be times when Jesus asks you to take a step of faith. That step of faith might look like changing jobs, changing friends, moving or even joining a ministry. Our faith grows when we choose to look to Him. For me, a step of faith I recently took was deciding to homeschool my three children. Homeschooling was something I had long desired to do. Now, after prayer and seeking wise council, my husband and I felt that God had given us a green light to start this new journey in our life.

Then, when we had started the homeschooling journey, we became extremely busy, and I began to second-guess our decision. The moment I would entertain the idea that we had made a mistake, I would become stressed and easily overwhelmed. I hadn't made that connection until the Holy Spirit showed me what was happening. I was shifting my focus from Him to my reality and allowing negative emotions to arise. In that moment, Jesus stretched out His hand to me through my husband. I needed support and encouragement that I had not made the wrong decision. I needed a support system that would keep me accountable and focused on what Jesus was doing rather than the reality around me. As soon as I shifted my focus back to God, I could feel the strength and faith rising back up in me to continue what He was calling me to do.

I'm currently in the process of learning to step out of the boat of my comfort zone again. This time I am stepping out in faith in another area of my life: my ministry of putting my heart into writing for you to see.

What wind or distractions has caught my attention, causing me to doubt and to have little faith?

_____

_____

_____

Who am I accountable to?

_____

_____

_____

Do I believe Jesus will send me a support system, someone who will encourage me?

_____

_____

_____

Sometimes our support and encouragement does not appear like we think it should. Be willing to keep looking and maintain an open mind.

What emotions do the distractions of my reality want to arouse within me?

_____

_____

_____

Jesus IMMEDIATELY saved Peter. Peter's faith had still been small in this area. He had focused on the wind and then felt the fearful consequences. Jesus responded to him by saying:

O thou of little faith, wherefore didst thou doubt?
Matthew 14:31

What was Peter doubting that had caused him to sink? Did the wind cause thoughts to flow through his mind? Maybe he doubted his ability to walk on water or doubted that the wind would not adversely affect his desire to walk on water. Maybe he had other doubts. Think about the following questions in relation to the situation you've been meditating about:

What is it that Jesus is asking me to do that will, in turn, take me out of the boat of my comfort zone?

_____

_____

_____

What is the wind around me that I am feeling?

_____

_____

_____

Am I focusing on the wind, which is my current reality, or on Jesus?

_____

_____

_____

Is there something in my life that I feel is bigger than Jesus?

_____

_____

_____

Now, think of the step of faith you are currently taking. You are stepping out of the boat of your comfort zone. You may feel the wind that is trying to shift your focus. When fear and doubt come in, you will find yourself starting to sink. For example, you may feel anxiety. If there is an area where you have little faith to stand strong, it's time to build your faith in that area.

The only way to build our faith in any area where we are weak is through the Word of God. I challenge you to grow your faith as you continue through this study, so that you are able to face your doubts and follow Jesus wherever He calls you to go.

Is God allowing my doubts to arise, to show me that I have little faith in a certain area of my life?

_____

_____

What network of guardrails and support can I have to keep me accountable to grab hold of Jesus' hand and continue to trust Him as I continue to step out in faith?

_____

_____

_____

What scriptures can I study and stand on that will build my faith in this area so that I will not have limited faith anymore?

_____

_____

_____

List below other scriptures that come to mind. You will come back to these scriptures at the end of the study, to continue your journey of stepping out of your comfort zone.

CHAPTER 2

EXAMPLES OF FAITH

By definition, faith is what you are hoping for that has not yet manifested in your reality! Hebrews 11 goes through great examples of faith, and we can learn from them. I want to take some time and think about the kind of faith some of the people in these examples had, starting with Abel.

ABEL'S FAITH
(A LOOK AT HIS HEART)

Genesis 4:1-7 and Hebrews 11:1-4

As I was studying in multiple translations, I came across this translation, and it really helped me fully understand Abel's faith:

> By an act of faith, Abel brought a better sacrifice to God than Cain. It was what he believed, not what he brought, that made the difference. That's what God noticed and approved as righteous. After all these centuries, that belief continues to catch our notice.   Hebrews 11:4, MSG

According to the Scriptures, it was NOT what Abel *brought*, but what he *believed* that made the difference. What he believed is what God noticed and accounted to him as righteousness.

If faith is what you *believe*, then Abel's offering was given in faith. Abel was not offering a sacrifice out of routine or a checklist of things he had to do to be a good follower of God. In his heart, he truly believed in what he was doing. Abel, therefore, is a good example of believing beyond what reality is saying to you!

God accepted what Abel brought to Him BECAUSE of the condition of his heart. Cain's offering was not an offering of faith, as was Abel's. God wanted Cain to search himself (see Genesis 4:6). God wanted him to look within his heart and do the right thing with the right motives. He did not.

What are the motives of my heart?

_____

_____

_____

If the motive of my heart is unacceptable, what is the Holy Spirit revealing to me that I need to change?

_____

_____

_____

Am I just going through a season of the motions, routines and habits of Christianity?

_____

_____

_____

If so, what is this season I am going through revealing to me?

_____

_____

_____

Do I truly believe in my heart that God will accept what I am offering to Him?

_____

_____

_____

An offering is a gift you give without expecting anything in return.

Do I believe God's promises and His Word, or do the expectations of my reality fight against me? And why?

_____

_____

_____

NOAH'S FAITH
(POSITIONING HIMSELF BEFORE GOD)

Genesis 6:14-7:17

Can you imagine building a huge ark on dry land because you believe it will rain and flood, but at the same time, you don't really know what to expect. The people of Noah's day had never seen rain before, and that makes it possible that what God was asking of him seemed quite drastic.

I want to compare Noah's faith from these different translations.

By faith, Noah built a ship in the middle of dry land. He was warned about something he couldn't see and acted on what he was told. The result? His family was saved. His act of faith drew a sharp line between the evil of the unbelieving world and the rightness of the believing world. As a result, Noah became intimate with God. Hebrews 11:7, MSG

Faith opened Noah's heart to receive revelation and warnings from God about what was coming, even things that had never been seen. But he stepped out in reverent obedience to God and built an ark that would save him and his family. By his faith the world was condemned, but Noah received God's gift of righteousness that comes by believing. Hebrews 11:7, TPT

Faith is believing what you cannot see. Noah believed what God told him, even though he had never seen rain before, and his faith displayed what he believed. His belief positioned him to further hear what God was saying.

Has God revealed my calling or my ministry to me?

_____

_____

_____

If so, am I walking in it, or do I feel overwhelmed, not knowing how to step in and move to the next level of my calling or ministry, thus stretching my faith?

_____

_____

_____

Do I position myself in a way that I can hear revelations or warnings from God?

_____

_____

_____

If not, what can I do to put myself in that position?

_____

_____

_____

Noah would not have been acting in faith had he not built the ark. His faith was revealed through his actions. It took a long time to build the ark. This was not a one-day act of faith. Noah didn't build on the ark for a month and then say, "I see no rain, so I'm going to quit. I don't want to waste my time on this." No, he kept building the ark because God had told him to do it.

Noah continued building the ark even when other people spoke against it, trying to discourage him. His faith showed through his lifestyle, and your faith shows through your lifestyle, through your day-to-day actions. Faith is acting on what you believe, not just talking the Christian talk.

Noah's faith was so strong and influential that his family followed him into the ark.

Do I truly believe in my heart that the Word of God is true?

_____

_____

_____

Noah believed what God spoke to him and obeyed His voice by building the ark. If I say I believe the Word of God in my heart, I must do what He is asking me to do.

Had Noah believed other's influence (his family or the members of the community), he quite possibly would not have finished building the ark.

In what area or areas in my life do I follow the influence of those closest to me?

_____

_____

_____

Do I need to separate myself from them, so that God's voice grows louder?

_____

_____

_____

What step of faith, that I may not fully understand yet, is God asking me to take right now?

_____

_____

_____

Abraham's faith
(*Leaving Familiarity*)

Genesis 12:1-9 and Hebrews 11:8-10

Abraham knew the LORD had spoken to him, and, I believe, he knew what he needed to do. He left his homeland with only a promise from God. He didn't know *how* things would happen; he just knew they would! This is what the Scriptures call stepping out in faith.

> *Faith motivated Abraham to obey God's call and leave the familiar to discover the territory he was destined to inherit from God. So, he left with only a promise and without even knowing ahead of time where he was going, Abraham stepped out in faith.*
>
> Hebrews 11:8, TPT

We all have promises from the LORD. Some of us have promises that He has personally spoken to us, while some of us may have received dreams, prophetic words or visions. Every promise in the Word of God is for each one of us.

The promise of God to Abraham came to pass in his lineage because he acted on his faith. He applied what the LORD had said to him to his reality. The Word of God is meant to be applied, both in our hearts and in our everyday life.

It is time to line our lives up with the Word of God and do what the LORD tells us to do, even when we don't see how it will come to pass or why it is even necessary. Abraham may not have realized *why* he had to leave familiarity as the LORD asked him to, and yet he obeyed and left all that was familiar.

41

BE DARING AND STEP OUT IN FAITH!

What is the LORD asking me to change in my life to line up with the promises He has given me?

_____

_____

_____

Which part of the Word of God do I try to change to fit my life?

_____

_____

_____

Do I allow my life to change to fit the Word of God?

_____

_____

_____

It was a big step of faith for Abraham to leave everything he knew and all those who respected him, heading toward a place where he would be a stranger.

Do I listen to the influences around me and stop going forward in God or even go backward?

_____

_____

_____

Or do I take the step of faith to be obedient to His Word, regardless of the opinions of others? If so, why?

_____

_____

_____

SARAH'S FAITH
(BELIEVING BEYOND WHAT YOUR EYES SEE)

Genesis 18:9-15 and 21:1-8

By faith even Sarah herself received the ability to conceive [a child], even [when she was long] past the normal age for it, because she considered Him who had given her the promise to be reliable and true [to His word]. So, from one man, though he was [physically] as good as dead, were born as many descendants AS THE STARS OF HEAVEN IN NUMBER, AND INNUMERABLE AS THE SAND ON THE SEASHORE. Hebrews 11:11-12, AMP

By faith Sarah received the ABILITY to conceive, even though she and Abraham were both physically too old to bear children. She didn't have the ability to make her promise manifest on her own. The King James Version of the Bible actually states:

... because she judged him faithful who had promised.
Hebrews 11:11

43

When she believed in God and what He had promised her, she received the strength, the ability and an open door for the promise to manifest in her reality.

When Sarah made the mental decision to choose to believe what God said rather than what her reality said, she opened herself up in the Spirit to pull that promise into the physical realm. Maybe she realized on a deeper level that God was capable because He knew she had laughed. She told herself, "God is faithful, God is capable, and God's Word doesn't return void."

God doesn't need your reality to line up to the promise so He can move in your life. God needs your heart and mind to believe in Him so He can change your reality to line up to His Word! Our reality is a by-product of what is deep in our heart (what we believe to be true) and what comes out of our mouth.

Think about what could have happened if God wouldn't have confronted Sarah about laughing. How could her day-to-day speech have been any different? Could she have spoken words that could have halted God's promise from manifesting? Could she have even influenced Abraham not to believe?

What physical aspects am I believing in more than what the Lord promises to me, causing limitations in my faith and ultimately stopping my promises from manifesting in my life?

———————————————————————————

———————————————————————————

———————————————————————————

ABRAHAM'S FAITH
(OBEDIENCE TO GOD'S INSTRUCTION)

Hebrews 11:17-19, Genesis 22:1-14 and James 2:14-24

This section of faith speaks so much to us. It can really make us think about what we believe and do and how we see God. Are our actions truly revealing our faith? The end of James 2:18 states, *"I will shew thee my faith by my works."* As this passage in James continues, it gives Abraham as an example of someone whose works revealed his faith.

The Scriptures say it was faith that enabled Abraham to offer Isaac when he went through that testing. I don't want to focus on why he was tested, but rather how he reacted during the test! As you read Genesis, notice that the Scriptures don't recount Abraham arguing or asking a million questions. God spoke, and Abraham started acting. Notice that Abraham didn't even tell anyone (including his wife or son) what God had shown him or why he was doing what he was doing. He was being as obedient to God's voice as he possibly could.

I personally love the faith in Abraham's works recorded in Genesis 22. He was asked to offer Isaac as a burnt offering. But there was a prophetic promise attached to Isaac, and Abraham had a decision to make (see Genesis 17). He told his servants who went with him, *"I and the lad will go yonder and worship, and come again to you"* (Genesis 22:5). This statement reveals his heart.

Abraham showed his faith THROUGH his actions of obedience, when God had called on him to sacrifice his son on the altar. How did his willingness to offer Isaac show his faith? His actions showed obedience to God's instruction at all costs. I believe Abraham also had faith and believed in the promise he had received through Isaac more than he believed what was physically being asked of him in that moment.

The culture that Abraham lived in practiced child sacrifice. Could this have been a test to see what Abraham truly believed about God and what God would ask of him?

What do my actions reveal?

_____

_____

_____

Am I willing to give my promise back to God?
If not, why do I try to hold on to it?

_____

_____

_____

If Abraham would have chosen to believe in the physical, only what he could see, that version of reality could have caused him to reason why he should or shouldn't be obedient when God asked him to sacrifice his son. He could have had thoughts like: "If I kill my son, there will be no promise, and that doesn't sound like God." He could have compared God's voice to his reality and reasoned that it couldn't have been God speaking to him. Or did he simply believe in who God was and what His Word said. God's Word never returns void at any point in our lives. I believe this was the clear choice that Abraham made.

Abraham believed more in God and what God said rather

than what appeared to be happening in the physical world around him. It may have looked as though Isaac would die, but Abraham knew that, in the end, Isaac must live. If not, God was lying, and God doesn't lie.

Abraham didn't just step out in faith; he actually put his faith on the line! Even if he would have killed Isaac, I believe he trusted that God would do a miracle and raise his son up again to life. That is a strong and deep faith, to be willing to give your promise back to God, believing that He will turn everything to your good.

Do I believe more in the physical that I can touch and see or in God's promises and His Word?

_____

_____

_____

Do I reason, trying to discern if it is God speaking or not?

_____

_____

_____

Do I test my beliefs against the Word to see if they are true?

_____

_____

_____

Am I willing to put my emotions, comfort, finances, etc. on the line? If not, why?

A PARENT'S FAITH
(FOLLOWING DISCERNMENT)

Hebrews 11:23 and Exodus 2:1-10

Hiding Moses may have looked like his parents were acting out of fear. According to Hebrews, they were acting out of faith when they hid him for three months instead of acting out of fear of Pharaoh's decree. To be honest, Moses' parents probably felt fear, but they chose to act in faith, believing that God would intervene. At the same time, even though they had faith, they could not flaunt their freedom. They used wisdom and hid Moses from Pharaoh.

Notice who Moses' parents were. They were both from the tribe of Levi, and from the Levites came the priesthood after the Exodus. This was the tribe that God allowed to move and touch the Ark of the Covenant, which was to carry His very presence!

Going against Pharaoh required faith in who God was and knowledge that God sees the bigger picture. God's hand was definitely on Moses, and it was because of His intervention that Pharaoh's daughter had compassion on Moses and allowed a Hebrew woman to nurse him and pour into his life until he was weaned.

Proverbs 22:6 tells us: *"Train a child in the way he should go: and when he is old, he will not depart from it."* The faith that God would intervene led Moses' parents to place him in a basket, not yet knowing how God would work it all out. Their act of faith paved the way for them to take care of Moses, their own baby, with permission

48

from Pharaoh's daughter, rather than in secret. They were given the opportunity to pour into Moses' life, when what was physically occurring said they should not have had that privilege!

You and I have this same opportunity — to pour into those around us. Or we can choose to do what society tells us. Following society over our discernment wouldn't be the type of faith Moses' parents demonstrated. The faith they displayed was them acting and following their discernment over the preferences of their current society.

Moses' parents became part of the priesthood, and the New Testament calls us to *"a royal priesthood"* (1 Peter 2:9). We have access to the same discernment Moses' parents displayed.

Do my actions follow godly discernment (my insight from God) or the fear of society (my own discernment and observations)? And why?

_____

_____

_____

MOSES' FAITH
(THE OPENING OF MANY DOORS)

Hebrews 11:24-29

Here we read several testimonies of Moses' faith. He took a stand with the people of God rather than being known as Pharaoh's grandson. Hebrews states, *"Choosing rather to suffer affliction with the people of God, than to enjoy the pleasures of sin for a season"* (verse 25); *"By faith he forsook Egypt"* (verse 27); *"Through faith he kept the Passover"* (verse 28); and *"By faith they passed through the Red Sea as by dry land"* (verse 29).

Moses' faith enabled him to do such things throughout his life. Faith empowered him to avoid sin because he looked at the eternal aspect and not the moment-by-moment feelings.

When they came to the Red Sea, the Israelites hit a wall. There was no way to escape Pharaoh and his army. Still, through Moses' faith and leadership, God was able to move! Faith is what created the open door that allowed the Israelites to cross the Red Sea as on dry land.

Maybe you find yourself facing impossible situations, and you feel as though you are up against a wall. Maybe you don't see the open door right now for you to cross into victory. Matthew tells us that God is in the business of making the impossible possible in all our lives. It's time to look at what Jesus can do rather than what our reality dictates as an option. Jesus isn't limited by our reality. He created reality!

Am I focused on God or on my "reality"?

_____

_____

_____

**What do I see and hear that can
influence my reality or focus?**

_____

_____

_____

**Do I have the faith that chooses God's Word, His
truth and His promises over my own emotions,
pleasure, family or friend's influence?**

Do I have the type of faith that separates my life from the world, empowering God to open mighty doors in my reality?

JOSHUA'S FAITH
(OBEDIENCE AND WORSHIP)

Hebrews 11:30 and Joshua 6:1-21

"By faith the walls of Jericho fell down" (Hebrews 11:30). The walls of Jericho fell because Joshua was leading the Israelites. In Joshua 6, God gave Joshua specific instructions on how to conquer the city of Jericho, although it had walls that were impossible to penetrate. He told Joshua how many days to march, how to march, and who needed to march first.

Joshua's faith was in God, not in the reality of what he was up against. I believe that Joshua trusted so much in God's Word that he KNEW if he did what God said to do, God would do what He had promised. He was obedient to God's instructions, and the result was that God's Word came to pass, and those "impregnable" walls fell down!

We all have walls and areas in our lives we can't conquer without God's help. Worshipping God is an important tool for our victory. Joshua sent out the worship team first, as he was instructed by God (see Joshua 6:8-16). Music is spiritual warfare! For days Joshua fought a spiritual battle until his victory manifested in the physical!

Our faith in God will eventually show up in our reality!

What do I see as worship?

_____

_____

_____

Find scriptures that define or describe how God sees worship.

_____

_____

_____

Is true worship part of my daily lifestyle? If not, why?

_____

_____

_____

How can I change my lifestyle to make true worship a vital part of it?

_____

_____

_____

What is God telling me specifically to do or change so that He can move in my life?

_____
_____
_____

Rahab's Faith
(Following Peace)

Hebrews 11:31

Joshua sent two men to spy out Jericho, and those two spies end up in the house of a woman named Rahab. Rahab was a prostitute living within the wall that served as protection for Jericho. She hid the spies, keeping them safe.

Rahab's faith in and fear of Israel's God saved her and her family. According to Hebrews, she received the spies with peace when faced with two options. She could have:

1. Operated through peace and hid the spies.
2. Operated through fear of what could happen and tried to save her own life by telling local authorities where the spies were hiding.

Rahab made a decision that she had peace with, even at the risk of being caught and killed by her own people.

Do I follow peace or fear? And why?

_____
_____
_____

RAHAB'S FAITH
(CHOOSING TO TRUST)

Joshua 2:1-24

As you read Rahab's story in the book of Joshua, you can see why she hid the two men. She said, *"I know that the LORD hath given you the land"* (Joshua 2:9). She had more faith in the Israelite's Lord God than in what she had been taught about her own gods. She told the spies that the inhabitants of Jericho were afraid of the Israelites and their God because of the stories they had heard. For instance, they had heard about the Red Sea parting for God's people and about the Israelites destroying the Amorites. These stories frightened them because they revealed a powerful God they had not known or understood. Rahab chose to believe in the God of the Israelites rather than fear Him.

Now, Rahab put her faith in the Israelites and their God and hid the two spies from her own people. In doing so, she put her life at risk for a God she had only heard of. But she had heard enough of the power behind the God of the Israelites to know that He was the true and living God. She was on her way to a new level of faith, and I have to wonder if she even realized it.

Just having faith in the Israelites' God wasn't going to save Rahab and her family. She needed to act on what she believed. Her subsequent actions and the oath she made show us her faith. As long as she was obedient, she could save more than just herself. When we exercise our faith in God and, as a result, things manifest, we affect more than just ourselves. Through the guidance of the Holy Spirit, we can influence our spouse, our children, our parents, our cousins, our friends, our neighbors, and even our co-workers.

All of Rahab's actions were the result of what she had overheard and believed to be true about the Israelites' God. Our actions, positive or negative, result from what we believe to be true about the LORD our God, and our obedience or disobedience to the LORD God affects more than just us!

What have I heard about God's character, while I haven't yet seen or experienced it for myself?

_____

_____

_____

Am I open to experiencing it, or do I fear it?

_____

_____

_____

If I fear it, why?

_____

_____

_____

RAHAB'S FAITH
(A WILLINGNESS TO OBEY)

James 2:25-26

Rahab's faith, choosing to follow peace, and her obedience to the deal she made with the Hebrew spies were all important parts of her story. Faith alone would not have saved her. Having peace but not following it would not have saved her. She also needed obedience!

The spies told Rahab exactly what to do the day they would come into the city. These were the conditions to their agreement, and they reminded her not to break her end of the deal they had made. Faith, peace and obedience were all needed. Rahab had faith because of the stories she had heard. She had peace with her decision because she trusted the men to keep the oath they had made because of the faith they had in their God. Finally, she produced acts of obedience when she hid the spies and gathered her own family to be saved.

Is my faith dead because I have no works connected to it? Or is my faith alive because I have acted on what I believe?

(If you can, give an example of what each would look like in your life.)

What if God asks me not to do something but, instead, to be patient? Do I wait in patience?

_____
_____
_____

What is God, through either an unction of the Spirit or through wise counsel, telling me to do or not to do?

_____
_____
_____

Am I obedient in doing what He is asking of me to the degree it is asked? If not, what is stopping me?

_____
_____
_____

When God places us in a position to grow our faith, we have two options:

1. We can be as the people of Jericho and fear what God says because we don't understand it.
2. We can be as Rahab, putting faith and action together, bringing us to a higher level of faith.

Which option do I find myself living in?

_____
_____
_____

Am I willing to put my faith in God, even if it may cost me?

If not, what am I not willing to risk?

JOSHUA AND RAHAB'S FAITH
(COMBINING OUR FAITH WITH OTHERS)

Joshua 6:20-27

The Israelites did just as God commanded Joshua. They marched around the walls of Jericho for seven days. Then, on the seventh day, they shouted at the sound of the trumpet, and the walls fell down.

The two spies who had made a deal with Rahab kept their part of the deal by going to get her and her family out of her house. They brought what they were commanded to the treasury of the Lord and burned the rest:

And Joshua saved Rahab the harlot alive, and her father's household, and all that she had; and she dwelleth in Israel even unto this day; because she hid the messengers, which Joshua sent to spy out Jericho. Joshua 6:25

Notice: Rahab's faith in the Israelites' God produced a harvest, not only in her life, but in her family as well!

James refers to faith without works attached to it as being *dead* faith. Matthew compares faith to a mustard seed with the ability to move mountains in our lives. Faith is activated in our situations when we act on it, producing a harvest in our lives and affecting those around us.

Look at Joshua and Rahab as a picture of faith. Joshua's faith in the Lord was revealed through the obedience with which he responded to what God had said, as well as by his honoring of the covenant the spies had made with Rahab. Rahab's faith was revealed through her actions when she hid the spies because of her faith from the stories she had heard. She also kept her end of their bargain by not telling anyone else about the Israelites' plan and not bringing anyone else into her house but her family members.

The faith of Joshua and the faith of Rahab combined produced a harvest, and that harvest was a new reality for Rahab and her family. Her faith had changed her environment and the environment of those she had a close connection with. Her act of faith changed her lineage for generations to come.

Where is my faith right now?

_____

_____

_____

Did I make a commitment to God somewhere and not fulfill it?

_____

_____

_____

Am I acting on my faith, activating it? Or is my faith dead faith?

Am I willing to join others to link our faith together if God tells me to, regardless of who it is?

If I am acting on my faith, what harvest am I reaping because of my faith?

Sometimes we may not see a direct harvest at the moment, but we can see others around us being influenced by our faith.

If my actions aren't lining up with my faith and what I am believing for, what changes do I need to make today to be more effective in aligning myself with the Word of God and His promises?

CHAPTER 3

SEEING THROUGH GOD'S EYES

Mark 4:35-41

Jesus and His disciples got into a ship, and then Jesus fell asleep. Then there arose a storm on the water, and when the disciples saw waves coming over the side of the ship, they started to fear that they would all die. They all began to look for Jesus and found Him asleep.

Am I facing a situation and feel as though Jesus is silent?

_____

_____

_____

The disciples woke Jesus up and asked Him for His help. Didn't He care that they were all about to perish? After all, they had been through with Him, how could He possibly just sit by while they drowned? Jesus wasn't bothered by all of this. He woke up, rebuked the wind and commanded the sea to be calm, and when He did this, the wind immediately stopped blowing, and the sea was calmed.

Jesus turned and asked the disciples, *"Why are ye so fearful? how is it that ye have no faith?"* (verse 40). Here we see that fear and faith are opposites. The disciples were focused on what they could see and feel, which was the reality of the wind and waves, and this reality they chose to focus on allowed fear to grip them. They woke Jesus up because of the waves, but notice that the first thing Jesus spoke to was the wind. They couldn't see the wind, but the wind was the cause of the waves.

We begin to fear when we focus on our reality, which is like them focusing on the waves. This begins to weaken our faith. Our reality may look like an impossible situation. We may feel as though we are drowning and can't take anymore. We tend not to look for the reasons behind our reality or why our emotions are going crazy. We may even spend our time talking to the waves and feel ineffective, and when we feel ineffective, fear can start to grip us.

Do I run to Jesus from a root of fear or from faith?

_____

_____

_____

Do I look and speak to my reality and my emotions? Or do I look behind them, asking Jesus, "What's the cause behind these waves?"

_____

_____

_____

After I have spent some time listening to Jesus, what is He showing me that is behind the storm in my reality?

_____

_____

_____

Exodus 14:1-31

Most of us have heard the story of Moses parting the Red Sea and the Israelites crossing over on dry land. Let's study the process of this miracle:

- The LORD told Moses that Pharaoh would follow the Israelites because he had a hardened heart.
- But, He said, through Pharaoh, the LORD would be honored.
- Sure enough, Pharaoh came after the Israelites with more than six hundred chariots.
- The Israelites saw the Egyptians coming close to them and were frightened.
- Next, the Israelites started complaining.
- Moses had to confront them and tell them: *"Fear ye not, stand still, and see the salvation of the LORD ... . The LORD shall fight for you, and ye shall hold your peace"* (verses 13-14).
- An angel of God stood between the Israelites and the Egyptians, being a cloud to the Israelites while being darkness to the Egyptians.
- Then came the parting of the sea with the Egyptians being destroyed.

The Israelites looked at Pharaoh and his army, questioned their faith, and started complaining. The minute they took their eyes off of what the LORD was doing and looked at their reality, they were given the opportunity to lose faith.

We are given the same opportunity every time we shift our focus from what the LORD is doing to what our reality appears to look like. When we are led by our emotions, our focus sways from faith to fear, causing us to begin to complain.

Moses had to confront their fears and remind them that the LORD was fighting for them. He helped the Israelites to get their focus back on the LORD and not the reality they could see at that moment.

Maybe you find your emotions rising, causing your faith to be tested. You may even experience fear because your surroundings, or the atmosphere, is intimidating you. You may have even started complaining and doubting whether or not your promise will come to pass. Maybe you are unsure if you will even make it out of the battle you are currently facing.

Am I focusing on the LORD or on the circumstances I see at the moment? And why?

_____

_____

_____

What in the physical makes me fear and doubt, causing me to lose my faith in the LORD in a given situation?

_____

_____

_____

2 Kings 6:8-17

Imagine waking up in the morning, looking around you, and seeing yourself surrounded by enemies. Do you ever wake up and find that everything seems to start going wrong? You had a bad morning, and that led to a bad day?

Elisha prayed for the Lord to open the servant's eyes so that he could see that the Lord's army was bigger than the enemy they were facing. But, before Elisha prayed for the servant's eyes to be opened, he told him, *"Fear not!"* (verse 16).

The servant had to get his focus off of the reality that was causing him to fear, for fear is the enemy's faith. 2 Timothy 1:7 declares, *"For God hath not given us the spirit of fear; but of power, and of love, and of a sound mind."* You can't have faith and see beyond a situation in your reality, and at the same time, operate in fear. Maybe God is allowing the enemy to stir things up within us to wake us up.

The Bible tells us to *"count it all joy"* when we go through various trials (James 1:2). The servant needed to shift his focus and believe in what Elisha was telling him more than he believed the reality his eyes were telling him about. Whatever we choose to focus on will feed either fear or faith. The choice is ours!

Once the servant shifted his focus, his eyes were opened, and he could see the Lord's army. We need to shift our eyes to the Lord instead of focusing on our reality. Romans 8:31 states, *"If God be for us, who can be against us?"* Are we focused on the Lord? Or are we focused on who we are? There are opportunities—health, prosperity, promotions, good friends and so much more—out there for us. The Lord wants to bless us beyond our reality, but we have to ask Him to open our eyes.

Are you content seeing only your reality as it seems to be, or do you want to see your reality from Heaven's perspective? It's time we shift our focus to see where the Lord is in our lives instead of where the enemy is!

Do I want to see my reality from the LORD's perspective?

_____

_____

_____

What fear stops me from seeing past my current reality?

_____

_____

_____

Am I willing to face that fear and ask the LORD to show me my reality from His perspective? Why or why not?

_____

_____

_____

Job 1:1-22

Job's character is described as that of a man who feared God and stayed away from evil. Then, we see God and Satan having a conversation. God brought Job's name up in the conversation. He didn't attack Job, but He gave Satan the power to do so. Notice that although Satan had permission to attack Job, God placed limits which Satan could not cross. Satan could not touch Job's life!

The attacks on Job started. He lost his servants, his animals, and his children. Let's think for a moment what these things could have represented to him. The animals were his way of living, the servants were those working for him, and his children were his family. He suddenly lost his family, those closest to him, his income, his food, and the way of life he had known. In a very short time, he went from prospering in every way to feeling as though everything was being ripped out from under him.

As soon as Job realized what was happening, notice what the Scriptures say he did: *"Then Job got up and tore his robe and shaved his head [in mourning for the children], and he fell to the ground and worshipped [God]"* (Job 1:20, AMP). Even though Job was still reacting to reality by mourning for his children, he still worshipped God. His faith didn't rest in his reality, and trials and storms didn't destroy his faith. Even after losing everything, something inside of Job still worshipped God!

Have the storms of my life—past or present— tried to destroy my faith because I am not deeply rooted in God through a firm foundation?

Do I continue to worship God, even when I don't understand what is happening around me, as things look their worst?

How are my circumstances affecting my faith right now?

Is my reality building my faith or tearing it down?

_____

_____

_____

Is my worship to God based on my emotions and the circumstances happening around me?

_____

_____

_____

Mark 1:16-20

Simon and Andrew were fishing when Jesus came on the scene and asked them to follow Him and become fishers of men. They immediately dropped their nets and followed Jesus. Then Jesus went down the road a little ways and saw James and John. They were in a boat, fixing their nets. Jesus called out to them, and they, too, left all and followed Him.

When Jesus called out to them, they stopped what they currently knew to do and responded to His call to make them *"fishers of men."* I wonder if they knew what being *"fishers of men"* meant. They didn't ask Jesus what it meant, how He was going to do it, or even how long it was going to take to accomplish. They simply responded to Jesus' call.

Many times, Jesus calls out to us to change seasons in our life, whether it is in ministry, friends, habits or routines. We naturally hesitate. Human nature tends to want to know *how* something will work out before we take a step of faith. We want to know the end result before we even decide to follow the direction being proposed. That is not acting in faith. Faith is taking the step when Jesus calls you. Faith is knowing and trusting that He has our best interests at heart and knows what He is doing.

When I feel a nudge from the Holy Spirit, do I immediately respond, or do I hesitate? And why?

_____

_____

_____

Do I weigh the cost?

_____

_____

_____

Notice, in these verses, that there was only one person who spoke, and that was Jesus! The Bible only gives us a short narrative of this event. It seems as though these four men only responded to what He was asking of them. What if Jesus says, "Pray for this person?" Do you respond? Do you reason out why it's not a good time, or why you don't think you need to pray at that moment? If Jesus calls you as a prophet or into a ministry you know nothing about, do you try to take every step He tells you to take? Or do you not follow His lead because of fear and uncertainty?

Do I try to understand the process of what Jesus is calling me to before I respond to His call?

_____

_____

_____

Following Jesus' call on our life can be scary at times because we have to allow Him to work through us by guiding our steps. It is not by our ability. If it was by our ability to do it, then it wouldn't take trust and faith in Jesus; we would have the faith in ourselves.

Do I trust and have faith in Jesus? Or is my trust and faith misplaced in myself or others? Why is that so?

_____

_____

_____

(If possible, give an example.)

_____

_____

_____

2 Chronicles 20:20 and Hebrews 11:1

"*Believe and trust in the* LORD *your God and you will be established (secure). Believe and trust in His prophets and succeed*" (2 Chronicles 20:20, AMP). We are told to believe in the LORD and also to believe in His prophets. Our belief is our faith. Our belief will limit how much God moves on our behalf. Matthew 13:58 says, "*And he did not many works there because of their unbelief.*" The minute we say, "This is impossible" or "This is never going to work," we have limited God. God can't do something in our life that we are not believing Him for. Our belief in the LORD establishes our life. What we believe, which is our faith, determines how we move when a storm arises.

Am I rooted in God's Word? And do I believe and speak God's Word over my circumstances?

_____

_____

_____

The second part of this verse says that our faith affects our reality. If we believe in God's prophets, we succeed. Why? Because we are choosing to believe God's Word over our reality! We are choosing to believe the promise He spoke to us through the prophets, through dreams, or in any other way, over the lies of the enemy! The prophets express the heart of God and His promises. They encourage us not to fold under the pressure of our reality. We are to *"war a good warfare"* through the prophecies spoken over us (1 Timothy 1:18).

As an example, if I believe God when He said in Romans 8, that He will turn the bad to good in the life of those who love Him, I have hope in my situation. Hebrews states that faith is what I hope for that I cannot yet see. If I choose to believe this, I will succeed and will be able to stand in the storm that arises because my focus is on Jesus. My faith is placed in Him rather than in the situation I face.

If I don't believe Jesus turns things to my favor, then I may begin to react to the storm through my emotions. I may try to defend myself rather than let God vindicate me. I may attempt to vindicate myself because I believe more in what I see and what others see rather than in what God sees or will do.

What step do I need to take to believe God and His prophets "more" than the reality I currently see and feel?

_____

_____

_____

Do I quickly dismiss prophecies or promises in the Word because of my unbelief when they seem impossible?

_____

_____

_____

Mark 5:21-43

Jesus was on His way to see a ruler's daughter who was at the point of death, when He was touched in the crowd by a woman who had suffered an issue of blood for twelve years. She said in her heart, "If I can touch Jesus, I will be healed." Then she went for an encounter with Jesus and didn't stop until she had touched Him.

This woman's touch caught Jesus' attention because He felt power leave Him. Her faith drew out the power of healing. Jesus told her, *"Thy faith hath made thee whole"* (verse 34). She received what she was going after because she had faith and didn't stop until what she was believing for had manifested in her reality.

Do I need to make a decision deep in my heart to not stop pushing through until I have an encounter with Jesus that changes my situation?

_____

_____

_____

In my situation, what would seeking Jesus look like?

_____

_____

_____

Do I see where my faith can change my perspective or my circumstances?

_____

_____

_____

Do I have faith as this woman did?

_____

_____

_____

Challenge: Seek Jesus for an encounter that will grow your faith and change your reality.

While they were still speaking, there came news that the daughter Jesus was on His way to see had died. Jesus responded: *"Be not afraid, only believe"* (Mark 5:36).

When they arrived at the ruler's house, Jesus allowed only three disciples — Peter, James and John — to follow Him inside.

He asked those who were mourning the young maiden's death, "Why are you crying? She is only sleeping." When they laughed at what He was saying, Jesus put them out and allowed only certain people in the room with Him. Why? Could it be that for the little girl's reality to change, unbelief had to leave the room (see verse 40)?

Does God need to get rid of some unbelief in me in order for my faith to manifest? If so, what unbelief?

_____

_____

_____

Matthew 9:27-29

There were two blind men who followed Jesus into the house, seeking a healing. Jesus asked them, *"Do you believe that I have the power to restore sight to your eyes?"* (verse 28, TPT). They responded with belief! They believed their healing was possible. Jesus' response to them was: *"You will have what your faith expects!"* (verse 29, TPT). Think about this simple truth. The healing of these blind men manifested TO THE DEGREE they believed and expected it to happen.

Do we believe and expect a change in our reality? If so, what would it look like? We may seek God for a breakthrough or a healing, but are we hoping for a change or expecting it to come a certain way or at a particular time? They had a momentary encounter with Jesus, and when He touched them, their faith's expectation manifested.

This is how we need to be with Jesus. When we seek a touch from Him, we should expect something in our life to change!

74

Sometimes, He changes our circumstances, and at other times, He changes us through our circumstances. We can pray for things in our life to change, but how are we praying? Are we praying from a place of hope and wishing, praying from a place of routine, and possibly being tossed back and forth? Or are we praying from a place of expectation and a firm foundation of faith?

What am I believing will change in my life as I continually encounter Jesus?

_____

_____

_____

How can I stretch my belief from hoping and wishing to a place of expectation for the impossible to manifest?

_____

_____

_____

I challenge you to pray from a place of expectation in your heart.

CHAPTER 4

MY SPEECH AND FAITH

Matthew 21:18-22

In this passage, Jesus cursed a fig tree for not having fruit on it. He was hungry, and sought some food, but there was none to be found. Later, the disciples asked Him, "How did you make the tree whither so quickly?" Jesus referred to speaking to the mountain and the mountain moving. He told the disciples that the cursing of the fig tree and the moving of the mountain were both accomplished by faith, and the power to move the mountain and the power to curse the fig tree were equivalent. He gave them the key to this kind of faith:

NO DOUBTING!

We have to get to the place where we truly believe and cannot be swayed. We need to get to the place where what we believe doesn't switch back and forth because of the influence of others.

Jesus emphasized this by stating, *"And all things, whatsoever ye shall ask in prayer, believing, ye shall receive"* (verses 22). This is a three-part process:

1. You have to ask God for something.
2. You believe you will receive what you have asked for in faith.
3. You receive what you have asked for.

What we believe and ask for will manifest in our reality when we receive it in our hearts. We will not ask for something and receive it if we don't truly believe in our hearts that we will receive that which we have asked for.

What am I asking God for?

_____

_____

_____

What is the mountain that I want moved?

_____

_____

_____

What mountain do I need to expose that causes me to sway back and forth because of the influence of others?

_____

_____

_____

Our words hold power. We are made in God's image, and God spoke the world into existence. Our words create or destroy, according to what we speak. We speak out of our heart. We want to speak faith and be positive at all times, but do we believe what we say? The Scriptures say that we receive what we have asked for IF we believe. We have to speak and not doubt what we say.

When you are in a place of authority, you have to believe others will listen to you. When you speak, you know the things you speak of will come to pass.

Look up the biblical definition of authority. What does it mean?

_____

_____

_____

Do I speak my faith with authority?

_____

_____

_____

Do I believe that when I command my reality to change, it will, the way Jesus commanded the fig tree to wither?

_____

_____

_____

If not, what mountain do I have that is stopping me from exercising faith with authority?

_____

_____

_____

(Notice: faith is linked with authority; you cannot separate the two.)

Mark 11:12-14 and 20-23

Here we see the same story, but from a different perspective. The next morning the disciples and Jesus were walking, and they saw the withered, dead tree. Peter had a thought as he remembered what he had witnessed. He got Jesus' attention and showed Him the tree. The fact that the tree had withered up caught Peter's attention, but it didn't surprise Jesus.

Why do you think Peter was so amazed at the tree withering up overnight from Jesus' words, when, according to Proverbs, *"Death and life are in the power of the tongue"* (Proverbs 18:21)?

_____

_____

_____

When Peter saw the manifestation of Jesus' words, it caught his attention. I think, personally, that Peter caught a new revelation of Jesus' power in that moment. Something transpired inside of Peter. He went from head knowledge to heart knowledge. Peter was amazed at the tree withering up and wanted to make sure Jesus knew it had happened. Jesus answered his amazement by telling Peter that he had the same power.

The Scriptures say that we are created in God's image and likeness. With this being true, our speech, through assured faith, dictates our reality, just as Jesus' speech dictated the reality of the fig tree.

Jesus went on to give an explanation of how the power and manifestation worked. He said, *"If you believe in your heart and don't doubt what you say, then, what you say you will receive."* Our words of faith manifest in our life when we truly believe what we say. This works both positively and negatively.

How is my speech toward the people and situations in my life?

_____

_____

_____

Am I speaking negatively or positively?

_____

_____

_____

Do I see my words manifesting and creating my current reality?

_____

_____

_____

What do I feel the Holy Spirit is telling me that I need to change in my daily speech?

_____

_____

_____

Luke 6:45 says, *"For out of the abundance of the heart his mouth speaks"* (NKJV). We speak what is in our heart. We may not get what we speak once or twice a week when we are sitting in church or talking with other Christians about the mountain we face because the speech the rest of the week, if negative, will overpower the positive speech. Our reality will manifest what we speak daily about the mountain because that is what we believe in our heart.

Think about it. If you planted a seed in the garden in your yard on Sunday and then dug it up on Monday to see if it was growing, then you replanted the seed but forgot to water it, what would you expect from it? If this is how you acted with a physical seed, would you expect it to grow or not? Why do we act this way with our words?

We all have a mountain we want moved in our life. Do we believe the mountain can be moved, or do we have doubt? Do we try to avoid the mountain by going around it? An example of a mountain we could face today would be sickness, financial difficulty, or anxiety about some issue.

What is the mountain I face?

_____

_____

_____

Do I claim the mountain I face (for example, "my sickness," "my debt")?

_____

_____

_____

Do I pray and believe for a healing or breakthrough, which would be the mountain moving, while, in the same breath, claim the mountain as unmovable with my speech?

_____

_____

_____

What do I truly believe and speak about the mountain I face?

_____

_____

_____

Do I apply what I hear and put it into practice (see Luke 6:46-47)?

_____

_____

_____

Matthew 13:53-58

When Jesus went to His hometown, the people there were amazed at what He was saying and doing, but, at the same time, they couldn't seem to get past who He was. They had grown up with Him. They knew His family and their history. Therefore, they couldn't receive from Jesus because of their unbelief. Notice: before it mentions their unbelief, it mentions the fact that they were offended. Offense will rob you! They were offended by Jesus.

Are you offended with Jesus and perhaps don't even realize it? When we are offended at a person, we are usually offended at Jesus as well. This offense creates our unbelief and limits what we can receive.

I'll give an example to help explain what I'm saying: Jane grew up in a very manipulative home. Everyone knew how or when to do things to get others to act to their benefit. They would act differently in front of other people than they did in the privacy of their own home. Every time Jane wanted to do something for herself, the permission she received came with a string attached. The only way Jane could get what she wanted was to do something for someone else. If there was nothing Jane could do to benefit them, then she would not get what she wanted.

What subliminal messages did Jane receive growing up? She may have started to believe that what she wanted didn't matter. She may even have felt that she wasn't loved because of who she was, but rather because of what she could do for others. This could have put her in work mode, and she may have become a people pleaser. Jane's value and identity became wrapped up in what she could *do* rather than who she *was*.

How do you think Jane's growing up affected her relationship with God? Because of the subliminal messages she was taught as a child, unknowingly, she could be serving God in work mode and not from a relationship stance. She may find her value in what she can do for God, and if she quits doing, then she may feel she won't be loved.

According to this passage in Matthew, these people limited Jesus because of what they saw in reality while they were growing up with Him.

**Do I limit the power of Jesus because of the reality
I have seen with family and friends growing up?**

_____
_____
_____

Who am I offended by and why?

_____
_____
_____

What if the person I am offended with is another believer? Do I unknowingly hold believers to a higher standard and fall harder if I am offended by them?

_____
_____
_____

How does that offense affect my relationship with Jesus (after all, He is supposed to be our Friend)?

_____
_____
_____

What offenses, unbelief, or lie do I retain that can stop miracles or healings from manifesting in my life?

_____
_____
_____

Mark 11:24-26

If we believe in our heart that what we are praying for is possible, then we will receive it. The passage goes on to talk about offenses that are retained in our heart. An example of a retained offense could be when we get annoyed with someone and choose to walk away. Later, someone mentions that this same person annoyed them, and suddenly our emotions are riled up again. We could be holding our offense in our heart without realizing it.

When we are praying and the Holy Spirit reminds us of an offense against someone else, we have a choice to make. We can forgive them or not. If we choose not to forgive them, it robs us of our prayers being answered. We can say we forgive someone and yet still retain a belief that causes us to stay guarded. We can forgive someone on the surface and still hold that offense against them in our heart. Or we can choose to forgive them and truly let the offense go.

We speak from the abundance of our heart. Everything in our reality can come from our speech. When we speak to our reality, which is like speaking to the tree, according to our faith, we get what we say. When we speak in faith about our reality, which is speaking in faith to the mountain we face, we position ourselves to receive what we have believed in our heart. When we pray about our reality, we are given the chance to see and change what is in our heart. When we pray about our reality, God shows us the connections that we must let go of for our reality to change.

What offense is the Holy Spirit showing me that I hold toward others?

_____

_____

_____

What offense is the Holy Spirit showing me that I hold toward myself?

_____

_____

_____

What offense is the Holy Spirit showing me that I hold toward Him?

_____

_____

_____

Am I willing to let go of the offenses the Holy Spirit is showing me and let God clean my heart so that my belief and speech can manifest with more power, changing my reality?

_____

_____

_____

Matthew 15:21-28

A Canaanite woman went after Jesus because her daughter was being tormented by a demon. Her faith was being exercised through a deliverance and breakthrough. She continued pressing toward Jesus, although she was being ignored and rejected ... until Jesus responded to her. She didn't give up! When we are ignored and rejected, we can easily become offended and stop seeking the Lord. The reality of this woman, even with the insult of being treated as a dog, could have been her justification for stopping where she was and accepting her reality as final.

Applying this to our life right now, when we are believing the Lord for a breakthrough, a mountain to move, or an impossible situation, how do we respond when we feel as though our prayers have hit the ceiling? Maybe we feel as though Jesus isn't hearing us. Maybe we know that He hears us, but we feel that He ignores us. Maybe we feel that other people receive answers to their prayers before we do. Maybe we feel that our prayers are impossible in the Lord's eyes. How do we get past these feelings? How do we endure until the point of receiving what we want? I believe the key is in the offense. As soon as the opportunity to be offended passed and the woman chose to keep going, her reality lined up with her faith.

Do I walk through potential insults and feelings of being rejected or ignored, to get past the offense and be able to see what I am believing for manifest in my life?

_____

_____

_____

Do I stop when I feel ignored, rejected or offended with Jesus or don't see my prayers being answered? Why or why not?

_____

_____

_____

Luke 7:1-10

A Roman officer had faith that Jesus could and would heal his servant. The officer sent Jewish elders to meet Jesus. The Jewish elders spoke highly of the Roman officer and suggested that Jesus might want to go visit his house.

As Jesus started in the Roman officer's direction, the officer sent friends to stop Him. This officer understood the chain of command and the line of authority. His understanding of authority was connected to his level of faith. Notice how Jesus responded to him. He said, *"I have not found so great faith, no, not in Israel"* (verse 9).

Our level of understanding and respect parallels with our level of faith! It is possible that the Roman officer sent the Jewish elders to Jesus so as not to cause any disrespect at Jesus' gathering between the Jews and the Romans? That, in itself, was a very high level of respect! The Roman officer also understood the power of words. As an officer, if he told someone to do something, he knew it would be accomplished. In that regard, when Jesus spoke, he understood that it was already accomplished.

Do I have a high level of respect for local authority figures, such as police, teachers, pastors, husbands, etc? If not, why?

_____

_____

_____

Do I try to undermine the authority over me when I see things differently?

_____

_____

_____

Do I submit to the authority God has placed over me?

_____

_____

_____

Do I understand the power of words—God's and mine?

_____

_____

_____

CHAPTER 5

MY HEART AND FAITH

Genesis 15:1-6 and Romans 4:1-5

Abram had a vision from the LORD and went on to ask the LORD about an heir. He had no children, only servants in his house. The Word of the LORD came to Abram and told him that he would have an heir. The passage continues, *"and he believed in the LORD; and he counted it to him for righteousness"* (Genesis 15:6).

There was no action that took place here, only believing in the Word of the LORD, but Abram's belief put him in right standing with the LORD God. Abram had faith in what the LORD was telling him, even if he couldn't see it in the moment.

When Abram was given this promise, he didn't know how it would come to pass. We all have the promises found in the Word of God for our lives. It is not true faith in the LORD God if we have already seen the evidence of how things will work out in reality. If it was, then our faith could easily be misplaced in the reality we see, instead of in the LORD God.

It is easy to see the possibility of an open door and to start putting our faith in the open door rather than in the LORD God.

Then, if the door closes, we lose hope and faith because our hope and faith was misplaced.

Is my faith placed in the LORD God? Or have I transferred my faith toward the reality that I can see?

_____

_____

_____

Genesis 16:1-16 and 21:1-5

Sarai was barren, and yet ten years later she found a way to have a child. In the custom of the day, if your handmaid had a child, it was still considered your child. Even though Ishmael was not born through the door the LORD had planned for the promise to flow through, the LORD still blessed him.

In Genesis 21, we see the promised heir arrive fourteen years later. That was nearly twenty-five years after the promise had been given. This was the LORD's undeniable door for His promise to manifest in their lives.

What might cause me to take matters into my own hands?

_____

_____

_____

How can I wait on the LORD instead of taking matters into my own hands, jumping ahead of Him?

_____

Revelation 3:7 refers to God opening doors in our lives. When God opens a door in our life, no other person will be able to close it. But when God closes a door in our life, no other person will be able to reopen it. Be assured that when God closes a door in our life, a new door opens for us to walk through.

Sarah had to live with Hagar and Ishmael in her reality because of a decision she made to help the promise come to pass. The LORD blessed Ishmael (her decision), but the consequences of that decision were still hard on Sarah. It was so hard on her that she treated Hagar badly, causing her to flee. We can create Ishmaels in our own life when we make rash decisions, instead of waiting on the LORD.

Have I created an "Ishmael" in my life, trying to ensure God's Word would come to pass? If so, do I now need His help to live with it?

Numbers 20:1-13 and 1 Corinthians 10:1-4

The Israelites were in the wilderness, and they grew thirsty. They started to complain to Moses, asking him why God would bring the congregation of the LORD into this wilderness to die? They wished they had died with their brethren (see verse 3). The LORD told Moses, *"Speak ye unto the rock before their eyes; and it shall give forth his water"* (Numbers 20:8).

Moses went before the people, but he hit the rock twice for water instead of speaking to it. This was not what the LORD had told him to do. The first time the LORD brought forth water from a rock when they were thirsty, it came through Moses hitting the rock (see Exodus 17:5-7). This time, the LORD wanted Moses to speak to the rock to receive water.

Perhaps Moses, knowing that what he had done the first time was successful, chose to do what he knew would work rather than stepping into something new. His action of hitting the rock instead of speaking to the rock was a form of unbelief. The LORD said, *"Because ye believed me not ..."* (Numbers 20:12). Jesus was in the wilderness with Moses and the Israelites, the same way He is with us in our journey.

Where do I become disobedient to what the LORD is asking of me because I rely and cling to my own strength?

_____

_____

_____

Do I choose to do things in God's strength? And how does that affect how others see God?

_____

_____

_____

In our daily lives, it is often easy to work out of our own ability rather than rely on our faith. Once we have been doing ministry or a certain ability for a period of time, we can easily start to rely on what we have learned rather than on the Holy Spirit.

We are limited by our belief system. In Mark 9, we see a man conversing with Jesus after bringing his child to Him for healing. The man told Jesus, *"Lord, I believe; help thou mine unbelief"* (Mark 9:24). This man obviously believed in Jesus' healing power, or he wouldn't have brought his child to Him for healing. So, where was this man's unbelief? Faith is what you are hoping for before seeing it manifest in your reality! In some areas, it is easier to step out in faith. In others, it seems harder and riskier.

Do I work out of faith in what the LORD tells me? Or am I working out of what I know already works?

_____

_____

_____

Those areas we struggle to have faith in will show us where we still rely on our own strength and ability. This is a choice we make. We can choose to trust and rely on God, and this causes our faith to grow.

Will I allow my faith to be stretched to step out in obedience when the LORD speaks to me?

_____

_____

_____

If not, am I limiting the LORD by what I believe or by what I have seen?

_____

_____

_____

2 Kings 4:1-7

This woman, who was now a widow, went to Elisha the prophet because she needed direction in her life. Her husband had died, and she was left with debt. The creditors were coming to get her two sons and use them as servants so that the debt could be paid. Elisha and the woman had a conversation about what her reality looked like. Elisha then asked her what she had of value in her home, and she responded, "Only a small jar of oil."

What do I have that is of value (examples:
time, finances, a vehicle, etc.)?

_____

_____

_____

Am I willing to trust what I value in God's
hands? If not, what would limit me?

_____

_____

_____

This woman was seeking godly counsel, and Elisha, at this point, started to give her direction on how to step out in her faith. He said to her, "Find as many vessels as you can. Then go home, shut the door, and pour oil into the empty jars from the small jar until all the jars are full."

What step of faith is God asking me to take?

_____

_____

_____

This woman left and was obedient to what Elisha had told her, filling every jar she had borrowed! She hadn't known what to do or what to expect. She was just being obedient to the direction she had been given.

In the physical, oil doesn't multiply this way on its own, but with God, all things are possible. God is not limited by our reality. All He needs is SIMPLE OBEDIENCE!

When the woman's son told her, _"There is not a one left"_ (2 Kings 4:6, AMP), referring to the empty vessels, the oil stopped multiplying in that moment. The minute this woman heard, "We have no more empty jars," the oil stopped. God multiplied the oil to the size of her faith and how much she had prepared for increase. This woman only had a small amount of oil, but she was willing to grow her faith. Through obedience, she used what she had. In the end, she had enough oil to pay off the debt that was owed and some left to live on.

Am I obedient to the direction I know God wants me to take? Why or why not?

_____

_____

_____

2 Kings 7:1-20

Elisha gave a prophetic word. The king's officer didn't believe it could happen, unless there was a window in heaven. Then, maybe it could have. This prophetic word gave a timeline. The word would come to pass by this same time the next day, and it did.

Am I like the officer and struggle with believing in the prophetic and the impossible? Why or why not?

_____

_____

_____

What things am I hearing or seeing that hinder me from believing that the impossible can happen?

_____

_____

_____

According to Isaiah 55:11, God's Word will not return to Him without results. His Word is not idle promises or threats. The officer who doubted this prophetic word wasn't able to see it come to pass, just as Moses wasn't able to see the Promised Land. God is the God of the impossible. When we doubt the Word, whether written or prophetic, we may not see it manifest in our lives.

We can use the prophetic words spoken to us for direction in our lives, while we can also view some words spoken to us as a breath of fresh air and hope. Some words may even be a warning of things to come. First Timothy refers to us using the prophetic words spoken to us in spiritual warfare. We are to remind ourselves of what was spoken over us and what is written in the Word for us. Then we can have hope and strength not to quit fighting.

Do I keep a written record of the prophetic words that are spoken to me?

_____

_____

_____

If not, start now. This could include verbal words, dreams or the written Word I am reading.

Do I recall these words by reading them and talking about them, keeping myself strengthened?

_____

_____

_____

Do I speak God's Word in spiritual warfare?

_____

_____

_____

His Word is the only thing that does NOT return without results!

John 4:43-54

Jesus was performing His second public miracle, again in Galilee, and we see what the Scriptures call _"a royal official"_ approaching Him. His son was sick and dying and needed a miracle to manifest in his reality. He asked Jesus to heal his son. Jesus responded: *"Except ye see signs and wonders, ye will not believe"* (John 4:48). This official continued to plead with Jesus to heal his son. Jesus later told him, *"Go thy way, thy son liveth"* (John 4:50).

The royal official believed what Jesus told him and started to head home. On his way, he was met by a servant who told him that the son's fever was gone, and he was now recovering. As the servant was talking, the man realized that the fever had broken in the moment when he had believed what Jesus was telling him.

We can say we have faith, but do we believe enough to act on that faith? This official's actions of obedience to return home showed that he believed what Jesus had told him. Do we truly believe in the Word of God enough to line the actions of our lifestyle up with it? Are we obedient to what Jesus tells us?

Think of something you have faith in. Maybe it's a promise, maybe it has to do with finances, maybe it's a healing, or maybe it's a situation with family and friends.

Do I say I have faith, yet find myself waiting for a sign or some type of evidence to show me that things are changing before I apply myself?

_____

_____

_____

Do I apply my faith with my speech and attitude as if what I am believing for has already manifested in my life before it actually does manifest?

_____

_____

_____

2 Kings 3:9-20

Here we find three kings headed toward a battle, but they needed water for their soldiers as well as for their animals. They wouldn't be able to fight well if the men and animals were dehydrated. They sought out a prophet, and the prophet told them to dig some ditches. Why would they dig ditches when there was no water? They must prepare for what they need. That was their faith. They believed they would have water, although they didn't know how. So, they were obedient and dug the ditches! Of course, their miracle manifested because their obedience through their faith opened the door for the miracle.

A few examples of digging a ditch could look like God telling you that you will have a baby, so, in faith, you start to prepare a nursery. If God speaks to you and says that an increase is coming, then you may start tithing like you have already received your increase.

Do I have any ditches dug in my life for my faith to manifest in? If not, what ditch can I begin to dig?

_____

_____

_____

2 Kings 20:1-13

The prophet Isaiah went to King Hezekiah and told him that he was dying and should set his house in order. When the prophet left, King Hezekiah cried out to the LORD, and the LORD heard his prayer. The Scriptures say that he *"wept sore"* (verse 3). Hezekiah cried out with begging and wailing, weeping bitterly to the LORD. The result was that the LORD had the prophet return to the king, to tell him that his prayer would be answered. He would have fifteen years added to his life! The Bible says: *"Ye have not because ye ask not"* (James 4:2).

What am I earnestly asking the LORD for in prayer?

_____

_____

_____

The king asked for a sign to confirm what he was hearing, and the sign he asked for was for the sun's shadow to go backward, and the sundial to move backward ten degrees. This time of the day had already passed, but the LORD did as Hezekiah had requested, signalling that time had been restored to him. He now had extra time because he had faith to believe in the impossible.

Mark 11:24 states, *"For this reason I am telling you, whatever things you ask for in prayer [accordance with God's will], believe [with confident trust] that you have received them, and they will be given to you"* (AMP). King Hezekiah's faith brought him healing and added time to his day and to his life.

Are we putting our faith out there? Do we believe that what we are praying for is even possible? That's our level of faith. It's harder to believe and have faith to be cured of a serious disease if we haven't tried to have faith for the healing of a headache first. It's hard to believe for debt cancellation and a miracle in finances if we haven't first used our faith to believe for some extra funds to pay off one bill.

At what level is my faith?

_____

_____

_____

Where am I applying my faith and allowing it to build?

_____

_____

_____

In what area has my faith become dormant because I don't step out in faith for the little things?

_____

_____

_____

We all have seeds of faith. We all have to start where we are and see things move in our lives, and our faith begins to grow. Our faith, small as a seed, can move mountains. We say we have faith that God is our God and that He does the impossible, but do we truly believe He can do the impossible?

Do I truly believe I will receive what I am asking the LORD for?

_____

_____

_____

If not, in what areas do I need to allow my seeds to grow?

_____

_____

_____

Matthew 17:14-21

The disciples exercised their faith and tried to cast out a demon, but they were unsuccessful. After Jesus cast the demon out, the disciples asked Him, "Why didn't we succeed?" Jesus responded, _"Because of your unbelief: for verily I say unto you, if ye have faith as a grain of a mustard seed, ye shall say unto this mountain; Remove hence to yonder place; and it shall remove; and nothing shall be impossible unto you"_ (Matthew 17:20). Their faith, once again, was connected to their beliefs.

When I exercise my faith, what area in my life do I feel unsuccessful in?

_____

_____

_____

We all have to face certain seasons in life. How do we learn to face those seasons and mountains rather than walk around them? We just walk around the mountains we face when we are justifying, defending, or giving an excuse as to why things are the way they are.

We need faith as a mustard seed! A seed is a living thing. With the right atmosphere and nurturing, a mustard seed produces a tree, and that tree has more seeds within itself to reproduce. If you need help believing that prosperity or a healing is possible, then get around people who believe that prosperity and healing are possible. They will help you to believe more than you currently believe on your own.

According to James 2:20, *"Faith without works is dead."* So, if we have faith that the mountain will move in our life, yet we don't line up our speech with what the Word of God says (by speaking to it, commanding it to move), then is our faith dead or alive? We say we believe, but are we willing to do what we are uncomfortable with?

For example, if I am praying for family unity, but I am hesitant to confront the situation, will my actions line up with what I am believing for? Remember, faith, as a seed, moves mountains. This is living faith. This is faith with actions! A seed breaks through when it is under pressure from within to sprout. Stepping out when we are uncomfortable could be the pressure that causes the seed of faith to break through and begin to sprout, changing our life forever.

Where do I struggle to believe it is possible for the mountain I face to move and the season to change?

_____

_____

_____

Mark 9:14-29

Mark tells the same story, but from a different perspective. Jesus walked up to a group who were talking with the disciples and inquired about what was going on. A man approached and asked Jesus if He could help his son. The son was *vexed* with a demon, and the disciples had been unable to cast it out. Jesus cast out the demon, and the boy was set free. There are two key points here with two different people that I want us to meditate on:

#1- The Disciples

- They were unable to cast out the demon.
- Jesus said that this kind of demon only comes out by prayer and fasting. This is not a one-time thing you do. Prayer and fasting is a lifestyle that gives you a deeper relationship and authority level with Christ.
- Isaiah 58:6 talks of fasting breaking things that have a hold on us.

#2- The Dad

- He was bringing his son to anyone who could possibly help him.
- His son's deliverance depended on how he believed. According to Romans 12:3, we all have *"a measure of faith."*
- The dad wanted to believe it was possible, but he had just watched the disciples fail. This failure could have made him doubt that his son's deliverance was even possible.
- The dad's response was: "Help me to believe that it's possible."

Jesus told the dad, *"If thou canst believe, all things are possible to him that believeth"* (Mark 9:23). Our belief limits how many miracles and breakthroughs can happen in our lives. God can do the impossible. He is not limited by our reality. He created reality! Do you believe that the impossible is possible?

What is my level of faith, and where do I struggle to believe?

_____

_____

_____

Do I ask the Lord to help my unbelief? What if the Lord wants to use someone along my pathway to help me (see Galatians 6:2)?

_____

_____

_____

If I don't ask the Lord to help my unbelief, why?

_____

_____

_____

When I pray or seek the Lord for an answer and the first attempt fails, do I give up or keep pushing until I get an answer or a breakthrough?

_____

_____

_____

Matthew 6:25-34

Jesus was talking about being worried and referred to the birds and the grass. He told us that they don't have to worry because God takes care of them. If God cares that much about the birds in the air, how much more does He care about us, for we are created in His image? He talks of worrying about what we eat, what we drink and what we put on our body. At the end of verse 30, Jesus referred to this as *"little faith."* You still have faith; it is just little faith.

The Message translation states it this way, *"People who don't know God and the way he works fuss over these things, but you know both God and how he works"* (Mark 6:32, MSG). According to this translation, knowing God and how He works stops you from worrying. We tend to worry about a situation, leading us to control because we don't have the confidence things will work out the way we want or expect.

There is a difference between worry and preparation. If we know there is something happening that is out of our control, we can prepare for the possibility. If we don't adequately prepare, then we leave room for worry to arise. If we adequately prepare, then we have faith that things will work out in our favor, even if we don't understand *how* God will intervene or how He will vindicate us.

Is there an area of my life where I struggle with worry but should be standing in faith?

_____

_____

_____

There is also a difference between "knowing" someone or "knowing of" someone. When we know someone, we know their heart, their character, their favorite color, their life story, their likes and dislikes. We may even know their favorite things to eat, favorite hobby or favorite music. This type of knowing comes from a relationship. When we truly "know" someone, we have heart knowledge or revelation of them.

If we "know of" someone, we know them from the stories we have heard of them or from others' experiences with them. We may know the characteristics and actions of the other person, but we will not know the secret things of their life or even their preferences. When we "know of" someone, we have head knowledge or surface information of that person.

In the place that I am worried about, do I "know" God, His characteristics, and how He will work in my situation? Or do I only "know of" God and His characteristics, through others' stories I have overheard?

———————————————————————————

———————————————————————————

———————————————————————————

CHAPTER 6

USING MY FAITH

1 Samuel 17:1-11

The Israelites were coming up against the Philistines, giants who seemed invincible. We all have a giant we must face in life. We all have a situation, a fear, or something so big that we don't think we have the ability to face and conquer it. An example of a giant we may face could be a health issue we battle, TV shows that we are addicted to, family members we are unable to confront but who take our peace away, an unbelief in an area where we struggle to truly believe something is possible or an unsaved spouse.

If you say that your mountain is a family member or an unsaved spouse, you need to realize: that person is not the enemy! Your mountain isn't truly the person, but what that person brings to the situation or the marriage.

The story starts out with the Israelites on one mountain and the Philistines on a facing mountain, with a valley in between them. Goliath walked down to the valley and began to taunt Saul and the Israelites, causing fear to grip them. All they saw was a giant taunting them. They didn't feel they could win if they tried to fight him. And they knew that if they fought and lost, they would become servants to the Philistines.

While in the valleys of our life, our low points, the enemy will taunt us the same way Goliath taunted the Israelites. The enemy will come up against us, trying to intimidate us. We may even feel that if we try to fight, we will lose the battle altogether. Have you ever caught yourself saying, "Why even bother?" Or "What's the use?"

What is the giant, the spiritual battle, in my mind that I hear taunting me?

_____

_____

_____

What are the thoughts the enemy is throwing at my mind?

_____

_____

_____

1 Samuel 17:12-27

Goliath came out and taunted the Israelites twice a day for forty days. The Israelites were not responding, but they were absorbing the fear and intimidation that was being projected to them.

What do I tolerate that causes fear and, therefore, causes me to go backward?

_____

_____

_____

Notice that David entered the scene out of obedience to his father. He heard the shouts of the battle and asked his brothers how they were doing. While they were talking, Goliath came out and taunted the Israelites again. This time was different. This time David heard him.

The men told David about the reward offered to anyone who killed Goliath. David responded, *"For who is this uncircumcised Philistine that he has taunted and defied the armies of the living God?"* (1 Samuel 17:26, AMP).

Wow! Look at the two different responses. The men of the Israelite army heard what Goliath said, and they saw a giant coming against them. David heard the exact same thing they had heard, and yet he saw someone coming against his God! What was the difference? The men of Israel's army had been tolerating and absorbing the taunting, which caused their souls to be vexed (2 Peter 2:8). David came in with a fresh, untainted outlook. The Israelites saw the physical battle in front of them, while David saw the battle that was unfolding in the spirit realm.

When I see and face the taunting of a giant, do I see reality, as the Israelite army did, and not know how to respond? Or do I see reality, like David did, comparing the giant to my God? And why?

_____

_____

_____

1 Samuel 17:28-30

As you read these three verses, you will see the brothers accusing David of coming to the battle for the wrong reasons. They claimed to know his heart and motives.

David seemed to be the only one not afraid of the giant. Now he was getting criticism and accusations from his brothers and the rest of the men of Israel. After talking with several people, he saw that their responses were the same.

When we try to face a fear or a giant in our life, we look to those we think are on our side for support. At times, we may indeed find support, but at other times, we can actually find discouragement.

When we are accused, like David, of having ulterior motives, it is hard to ignore the words we hear and still face our giant with confidence. If we aren't careful, we can allow those words to dictate our actions and the direction we walk in. Words are very powerful.

As I face accusations, like David did, am I strengthened in my perspective of the giant's accusations and battle against God? And do I, therefore, go to battle?

_____

_____

_____

Or do I listen to the words and criticism around me from those tolerating the influence, ultimately changing my perspective?

_____

_____

_____

1 Samuel 17:31-37

King Saul heard them talking and tried to discourage David from going up against Goliath. The king was the leader of the army and the ultimate authority over David in that moment.

I love David's response to the king. He told him, "I used to keep sheep, and I defended them against a lion and a bear. If God could help me with the lion and the bear that wanted to attack my father's sheep, then He will deliver me from the hand of the Philistine as well." Saul then gave David permission to go to battle.

First, David received criticism from his peers; now he received criticism from the authority over him. Notice that David was not disrespectful when he put God in the middle of the situation, as he confronted the authority figure over him.

Saul was looking at the physical aspects only. He was looking at the age of Goliath and how long he had been a warrior, while David looked at the physical aspects in comparison to his God. David chose to see the lion and the bear and how God had moved on his behalf. He, too, could have gotten discouraged, but he chose to remember and talk about his past victories, building his faith and Saul's faith for the battle he faced against Goliath.

When I am getting discouraged, what past victories in my life can I use to build my faith and the faith of others around me?

_____

_____

_____

Am I a David in my situation, fighting off criticism? Or am I the one giving the criticism?

_____

_____

_____

1 Samuel 17:38-39 and Ephesians 6:11-18

Saul prepped David for battle by putting his armor on the lad. David secured his sword and then tried to walk around. This is an extremely significant point.

Our sword is the Sword of the Spirit, the Word of God. All the pieces of the armor of God are linked to the Word. The truth, the Word of God, is the belt. God's righteousness covers our heart. God guides our steps through His peace. Our faith, what we believe, either blocks the darts of the enemy or allows them to pass through. And then there is the helmet of salvation.

This armor is specific to each person. It goes according to OUR OWN revelation in the Word! David could not walk in or fight the giant through Saul's revelation. He needed his own armor. He needed his own revelation.

Think about the revelation of God David already had. He knew God through his experiences with the lion and the bear. So, how did he fight Goliath? The same way he fought the lion and the bear. That was David wearing his own armor and going against the giant through his own revelation of God, what he personally knew to be truth.

We cannot go against our giant according to someone else's revelation of the Word. We cannot conquer our giant with our pastor's, our parents', our spouse's, or even our friend's revelation of the Word. We need to seek God for a personal revelation

116

of Him today. We must go to battle with our own revelation of who God is for us and in us.

Am I winning or losing the current battle?

_____

_____

_____

Am I leaning on another's revelation of God and the truths they believe for my battles?

_____

_____

_____

Do I need a deeper revelation of the Word and of God for myself, as I go against this giant that I currently face?

_____

_____

_____

What support do I surround myself with when I go to battle?

_____

_____

_____

1 Samuel 17:40-58

David collected five smooth stones, put them in his bag and went forward to meet Goliath. Notice that when Goliath saw David, he started to criticize again. David wasn't worried about the criticism or what the enemy was using against him in the battle. He knew who was fighting for him.

David knew what God was capable of because of his experiences. God showing up and enabling him to defend his father's sheep he was tending to formed a foundation of heart knowledge of God's character inside of David. That heart knowledge allowed him to let God fight through him and conquer the giant he was currently facing.

Sometimes God will place people in our lives as a support group. David didn't have a support group; he had to rely solely on God to back him up.

When I am facing a giant, do I face him in my own strength or through the name of the Lord through a revelation I have received?

_____

_____

_____

Joshua 1:1-9

When Moses died, Joshua took over as the leader of the Israelites. The LORD spoke to Joshua and told him, "Everywhere your foot touches the land, I will give it to you." Joshua would have to cross the Jordan River to get new territory for his people. The LORD went on to tell him to be strong and courageous.

In verse 7-8, the LORD laid out a formula for Joshua to be successful in every battle he faced, whether in that moment or in the future. Joshua was a sure winner! What was it the LORD told Joshua?

1. Observe the Law Moses commanded.
2. Don't turn to the right or the left. Don't compromise! Don't do a version of your own interpretation of the Law.
3. Don't stop speaking the Word of God.
4. Meditate on the Word of God, which is the Law, day and night, so that you know what is expected of you.

If Joshua abided by these things, he would prosper and have good success wherever he went. Regardless of the enemies he faced in the future, he would always conquer. We can line our lives up with these same principles and have success when we face any enemy. God doesn't promise that we won't go through challenges, but when we do, we need to keep these four observances as well.

Am I preparing myself now for what lies ahead?

_____

_____

_____

Out of the four steps the LORD gave to Joshua, which of them do I need to work on in my life most? And why?

_____

_____

_____

Joshua 1:10-18

Joshua went throughout the Israelite camp telling the people to prepare to cross the Jordan to claim the land as the inheritance the LORD their God had promised them. He said, *"Prepare provisions for yourselves"* (Joshua 1:11, NKJV). They only had three days to prepare food for themselves for the battle that lay ahead.

Notice that Joshua and others were only preparing food for themselves. It was their personal responsibility to prepare for themselves. For the Israelites to take possession of what the LORD their God had promised them, they would have to prepare enough food to sustain them. They would have to cross over what was standing in their way.

Are we spiritually eating the Word of God enough to prepare ourselves to go through a battle? Are we searching for an encounter with the LORD God that will give us the heart knowledge we need to sustain us for battle? We can't go around the enemy the same way the Israelites couldn't go around the Jordan River. We have to cross over and face the enemy currently standing in our way.

Am I preparing for battle, or do I just coast through life?

_____

_____

_____

When a battle hits me in the face, do I realize that I am unprepared? If so, what can I do to start preparing?

_____

_____

_____

What does my "Jordan River" (the first obstacle in my life) look like that I must cross over to face my battle head on?

_____

_____

_____

Joshua 3:1-5

Joshua brought the Israelites to the Jordan River, and they stopped there for three days. On the third day, he told everyone to follow the Ark of the Covenant of the LORD God. They were preparing to cross the Jordan, to start conquering the land and taking possession of their promise. There is a Jordan (obstacles, spiritual warfare, and resistance) in all our lives that we have to cross over in order to conquer new ground (the promises or prophecies we have been given).

There were precise instructions the people were to follow on distance and how to cross the Jordan. They were not to cross UNTIL the Ark showed up on the scene. Following the Ark was symbolic of us following the leading of the Spirit in our lives. We should be Spirit-led whenever we move from our current position. We cannot move until the LORD God shows up. Even though the people had instructions, instructions alone didn't guarantee success.

Do I wait for the Holy Spirit to lead me in His timing to cross the Jordan? Or do I try to cross the Jordan on my own?

_____

_____

_____

"Then Joshua said to the people, 'Sanctify yourselves [for His purpose], for tomorrow the LORD will do (miracles) among you' " (Joshua

3:5, AMP). The people were to ceremonially and morally make themselves clean before the Lord. They were to set themselves apart. They were to prepare and dedicate themselves in advance for the LORD God to move in miracles.

Just having someone give wise counsel or a prophetic word over our life isn't enough direction. We must cleanse our heart before God. It is time to prepare a place for the LORD God to move in our life!

An example of cleansing our hearts before God may look like letting go of offenses (there is a difference between surface forgiveness and true forgiveness from the heart) and letting go of beliefs we hold, the things we think we know.

Am I sanctifying myself, cleansing my heart today for God to move tomorrow? Why or why not?

_____

_____

_____

What area of my heart does the Lord want to clean out?

_____

_____

_____

Joshua 3:6-17

Joshua received a command from the LORD and then told the Israelites the plan. The minute the priest stepped into the water, the Jordan River would part, and the LORD God would lead the way for the people by the Ark of the Covenant. When the priests' feet hit the edge of the water, they were to stand still. They were not told to command the water or do any other action, just to stand still.

Water represents emotions and the Holy Spirit. Emotions will arise in tough times, and we have to remain calm and be obedient to the Spirit's leading. We have to respond to Him and not react to the waters.

The parting of the waters was to help the people get across the river safely, as well as for encouragement. It was meant to build their faith in the Lord God, so that they knew in their heart that He would drive out their seven enemies. We carry the presence of the Lord with us into every situation.

We are obedient to the Lord God when we do what He has told us to do. We stop when He tells us to stop. We move or speak when He tells us to move or speak. Waiting on the Lord God offers Him room to move in our life. When we walk into a situation, carrying the presence of the Lord and being obedient to everything the Lord God has said to us, we will see the Lord God part the waters of our life, allowing us to walk across on dry ground! We will find ourselves walking through a situation and not losing our peace. We will come through unharmed.

Waters can be the situations we face that cause emotions to rise, and we start to feel incapable of making it through. An example of waters we may need parted could be a sickness, a financial crisis, disunity in the family, or a fear that taunts us.

What adverse situation or situations am I facing?

_____

_____

_____

**What has the LORD God specifically told me
to do in the midst of my situation/s?**

_____

_____

_____

**Am I being obedient to Him and doing
what He said? Or am I reacting out of my
emotion to bring me instant comfort?**

_____

_____

_____

Joshua 4:1-24

"And it came to pass, when all the people were clean passed over Jordan, that the LORD spake unto Joshua" (Joshua 4:1). The Israelites did what Joshua asked of them, and obedience positioned them for the LORD to speak to them. We all want to have the LORD's voice direct our path, but are we doing the last thing He told us to do? The Israelites did the last thing He told them to, and the LORD moved so mightily they were able to cross the Jordan River on dry ground!

The river had stood between them and their advancement to the next part of their journey. As soon as they had crossed it, while the riverbed was still dry, they were told to gather a stone for each tribe and carry it to the place they would spend the night. There they were to make a memorial out of these stones, as it states in verse 6. The stones were to be a memorial, a sign, their testimony, their story of what the LORD had done for them.

As we cross through various situations in life, we are also to collect memorial stones. These stones we collect will cause our children and others around us to ask, "How did that happen?" We can then tell them the testimony and glorify the Lord.

Examples of some of the stones in my life that have become testimony, giving the Lord full glory for bringing us through the river we faced, would be:

- Two of my children were instantly healed of food and candle allergies.
- Anger and temper tantrums in one of my children stopped instantly, causing others to notice a drastic change in behavior.
- One of my children faces a hereditary eye disease. Her eyes are not supposed to get better without surgery, but only worsen as time passes. Her eyes are slowly improving and amazing her doctors. She is no longer a candidate for surgery, even if it was something she wanted. We have not seen the complete healing manifest yet, but we are watching the Lord move on her behalf.

What does my river look like?

_____

_____

_____

When I take my first step to cross that river, am I victorious? If not, do I ask the Lord what to do and stop until He speaks?

_____

_____

_____

Once I go through my river and am victorious, what's the stone I take with me as a testimony to others of what God has done for me?

_____

_____

_____

Have I shared my testimony with others? If not, why not?

_____

_____

_____

Joshua 5:1-9

The Israelites had crossed the Jordan River, seen the LORD do miraculous things on their behalf, and now had forty thousand men prepped for war. They were headed toward their first city to conquer—Jericho. Suddenly the LORD stopped Joshua and told him to circumcise all the men.

Circumcision was a custom God had commanded the Israelites to perform whenever a male child reached the age of eight days. These scriptures explain that after they had left Egypt, the men of fighting age died in the wilderness. They couldn't make it to the Promised Land because they had not obeyed the voice of the LORD. Now, those remaining in the wilderness, who wanted to fight for the LORD needed to be circumcised.

In the physical, circumcision is the cutting away of the foreskin to prevent infection or irritation from occurring. In the New Testament, we are told to circumcise our heart, but what would that look like? When we are saved, we leave our Egypt, which is a place of bondage, we go through the wilderness part of our journey, in which we want the promises of scripture to start manifesting in our lives. The Lord moves on our behalf, and we see miracles time and time again, as we progress in our walk with Him.

There comes a time when we are to stop and circumcise our heart. We have to cut away the walls we erected to hide our hurts from the past. These walls of self-protection we have put up keep those hurts buried deep in our heart. Through circumcising our heart, we allow the hurts to be exposed, and the healing process can begin. We expose the lies we believe and the misconceptions we harbor, and we make ourselves vulnerable before the Lord.

We stay in this part of our walk with the Lord until we are whole and healed in this area. Then we continue our walk with Him ... until He stops us to deal with a different wall we have erected in a different area of our heart.

Have I circumcised my heart, allowing the deep hurts and wounds I suppressed to begin to heal? If not, what is stopping me?

What walls do I need to tear down in order to let the Lord into those suppressed areas of my heart?

Joshua 5:13-6:19

Joshua saw an angel, captain of the Lord's host, and the LORD spoke to him and gave him a command. The LORD told him what, how and when to do certain things so he would conquer Jericho, the first city in the Promised Land.

Joshua gave the rest of the Israelites instructions on how to march around the city. He told them that once the walls were fallen, and they were in the city, they were to allow Rahab and her family to live. He went on to tell them NOT to take any plunder from Jericho. The city was consecrated to the LORD, for it was the first city they would conquer. Could this have been the Israelites' tithe to the Lord?

God warned them that if they took anything, they would bring a curse upon themselves and upon the whole camp of Israel. When we go into battle to gain ground from the enemy, the LORD will give us specific instructions. Even though we don't see the LORD telling Joshua exactly what to do with the plunder in Jericho, I believe Joshua knew what the right thing to do with it was. The Spirit guides us and convicts us, and, therefore, we know the right thing to do, as we listen for His still, small voice.

What are my instructions from the LORD? And am I being obedient to them?

_____

_____

_____

If I am not fully obedient to the things the Spirit has told me to do, what is He warning me about?

_____

_____

_____

Joshua 7:1-12

The Israelites had just conquered Jericho, a city they would not have been able to penetrate in the natural. They knew this victory had come only because of the Lord being with them. They now sent spies out to see about the city of Ai, preparing for the second battle. According to what they could see, they assumed that Ai would be easier to conquer than Jericho. Therefore, Joshua decided to send only a few thousand soldiers.

These men went out to conquer Ai, but they ended up retreating and losing the battle. This caught Joshua off-guard, and he fell before the Ark of the Lord. Basically, he asked the Lord, "Why bring us this far, only to let the Amorites kill us? We could have stayed on the other side of the Jordan and lived a contented life." He even went so far as to be concerned about what the Canaanites would think of the Israelites and their Lord after they had heard the rumors of them being defeated and chased off by the men of Ai.

Notice that Joshua did not ask the Lord for a battle plan, as he had with Jericho. He took what the spies said at face value and then acted on it with his own plan. It was not until they had lost the battle that Joshua asked the Lord why.

Do I go to battle with or without asking the Lord for His battle plan?

_____

_____

_____

Do I think Joshua was more worried about his own reputation or God's? What about me?

_____

_____

_____

The LORD told Joshua why they had lost the battle at Ai. It was through their disobedience during that first victory! After we overcome the enemy in one area of our life, it is easy to go on to the next area ASSUMING that we will be victorious again and that we know what we are doing. It is important that we seek God and hear what He says for each individual battle. It is equally important for us to seek the Holy Spirit's leading—regardless of whether we win or lose the battles we face.

It's possible to lose a battle and just go on with life, assuming that we probably should not have fought that battle in the first place and perceiving that as a destined reality instead of inquiring as to why we lost. There is importance in asking the LORD why we have lost any battle and then TRULY LISTENING to His answer. We may not always like the answer we hear, but if we listen, He will prepare us for the next battle.

If I am losing the current battle, do I ask the LORD why? Or do I accept the loss as my destined reality and continue to live defeated by the enemy? Why or why not?

_____

_____

_____

Joshua 7:13-26

Going to the LORD after every battle with an open mind is a must! Joshua went to the LORD and asked, "Why?" God responded, "Cleanse your heart today for tomorrow and go through the tribes. When you find the person who is disobedient, he is to be burned with fire." If they chose not to deal with this disobedience, they would not be able to face their enemies and be victorious.

A man named Achan confessed to having taken the accursed things out of covetousness. As a result, Achan and his family were all taken and destroyed. In this way, the Israelites purged the disobedience from their midst.

Do I sanctify my heart, honestly searching and cleaning it out, before the LORD?

_____

_____

_____

Am I honest with myself and others?

_____

_____

_____

Notice that it was not only Achan who was burned. His family, his animals, and all that he had were destroyed with him. What would have happened if his children would have lived? It is very possible that they would have repeated their father's actions out of learned behavior. The Israelites destroyed Achan and anything and everything attached to him.

We should be constantly cleansing our heart before the LORD. We should be confessing, not only what we have done, but also WHY we have done it. But are we truly willing to look at the deep things rooted in our hearts? It is through the Refiner's fire that these things are purged out of our lives. We must be willing to let go of all the connections that led us to compromise in our heart, or we haven't truly dealt with the issues at hand.

Do I allow ALL the connections and strings that cause me to compromise in my life to be burned out of my heart or not? Why or why not?

How does the compromise in my heart affect those around me?

Joshua 8:1-35

I love how this chapter begins following the Israelites' purging of themselves. *"Now the LORD said to Joshua, 'Do not fear or be dismayed (intimidated). Take all the men of war with you and set out, go up to Ai; see, I have given the King of Ai, his people, his city, and his land into your hand'"* (Joshua 8:1, AMP). They had lost the battle of Ai, but then they had cleansed their heart before the LORD with an honest evaluation, and now it was time to face the city of Ai again. It's easy to fear or be intimidated when facing something we previously failed at. We may hear the thoughts of failure that whisper in our ears. We may feel like it will be a repeat of the first time we went to battle and lost.

The LORD told Joshua that he would win this battle, just as he had with Jericho, and this time the Israelites could keep the spoil. The LORD gave Joshua a battle plan, an ambush, and told Joshua exactly what he needed to do to win.

Joshua told the Israelites, and the Israelites obeyed. They faced Ai for the second time, but this time they were victorious.

Am I seeking the LORD for a battle plan for each specific struggle I face? If not, why not?

_____

_____

_____

Do I recognize and admit what my struggles are?

_____

_____

_____

Do I make a plan, and when I'm in the middle of enacting my plan, ask the LORD to bless that plan?

_____

_____

_____

Notice the difference in the battle plans that both led to victory. In Jericho, the first city which they conquered, they marched around for seven days and then shouted, and the city was theirs. Ai, the second city conquered, was different. They first attacked and lost. They prayed as to why they had lost the battle. They realized their disobedience and where compromise had occurred and made it right with the LORD. Then, they received a new battle plan, and this battle plan included an ambush.

Am I ready to obey the LORD, follow His plan, and face my challenge again? If so, what is He telling me?

_____

_____

_____

Ask the Lord for a scripture, a song or a word you can stand on, keeping you encouraged.

Joshua 9:1-15

Here we see the third group of people the Israelites needed to conquer, the Hivites or Gibeonites. Two things stand out to me about how this particular conversation occurred:

1. Joshua asked a question. "Who are you and where do you come from?" (see Joshua 9:8). Notice that the Gibeonites deceived him with their response, while, at the same time, never really answering his question.
2. The Israelites received the things the Hivites had brought and made a peace treaty with them without asking the LORD (see Joshua 9:14).

Joshua didn't receive a direct answer from these people, but was caught up with their story, to the point that he made a peace treaty with them. He didn't consult the LORD before making this treaty, asking if he should or shouldn't make such a treaty. He made a decision based on the story he had heard and the emotions he felt in the moment. Joshua failed to seek the LORD for discernment in this situation.

The LORD is concerned with every minute detail of our lives. We can be deceived by what we see and hear in our current reality, and we must not fail to take each thought into prayer!

Do I hear the story of other people's lives and want to help or get involved without first asking the LORD if I should? Why or why not?

_____

_____

_____

Do I make impulsive decisions based on emotions I feel when I hear others' life stories and what I feel in the moment?

_____

_____

_____

Do I react to what I see or hear? Or do I pray about things, asking if what I see and hear is the truth?

_____

_____

_____

Joshua 9:16-27

Here the truth of the Gibeonites was exposed. Joshua learned that they did not really live far away as they had claimed. He had been deceived. The Gibeonites had heard about what was promised to Moses and acted out of fear. They had deceived and manipulated the Israelites into a peace treaty. According to verses 22-23, the Gibeonites beguiled the Israelites, and thus brought a curse upon themselves.

This word *beguiled* also appears in Genesis 3:13 and 2 Corinthians 11:3 in reference to the serpent and Eve. *Beguile* means "to betray, trick, deceive or mislead."[3]

The Israelites had been deceived and betrayed by the Gibeonites, but because Joshua had made a treaty with them, he kept his word and did not kill them. He had reacted without praying when he made the treaty, and he would now have to live with the consequences of his actions.

Think about the Gibeonites. They were now living under a curse because of their actions. They purposely planned to deceive and manipulate the Israelites because of their fears. Here we see the outcome of living two different ways:

1. We can act as Joshua did, making decisions without praying and based on what we see and hear. We can go to the LORD when we fail, asking Him why. Yet, we still find ourselves living with the consequences of the impulsive decisions we made.

2. We can do what the Gibeonites did, acting out of fear rather than faith. We may think we are making sure we are protected, by controlling the situations we face, to get what we feel we need, rather than believing God to protect us. We can self-protect through deceit and manipulation and live under the consequences of a curse due to our own actions.

_____
3. *Strong's* H#7411

In my everyday life, do I tend to act as Joshua (making impulsive vows or commitments) or the Gibeonites (making a Plan B and self-protecting)? And why?

_____

_____

_____

If you can, give an example of each.

_____

_____

_____

Joshua 10:1-21

Some kings heard what the Israelites had done to the two cities, Jericho and Ai, and they got together and planned to go after the Gibeonites because they had made a peace treaty with Joshua and the Israelites. The Gibeonites told Joshua what was going on, and Joshua and the Israelites agreed to help them in their battle. God told Joshua, _"Fear them not: for I have delivered them into thine hand"_ (Joshua 10:8).

Joshua went to battle with confidence and bold faith, having no doubt that the LORD was with them. He knew he had heard the LORD speak directly to him about this specific battle.

Do I have a clear word from the LORD for my life today?

_____

_____

_____

Joshua had no doubts about winning this battle. He had complete faith in the LORD. But, as they were fighting, Joshua realized they were running out of time. He could have had thoughts such as: "If it gets dark, we might lose this battle." He spoke to the LORD in front of the children of Israel. Then he commanded the sun and moon to stand still, and the LORD did what he was saying. The sun and moon stopped in their tracks until Joshua had won the fight. According to scripture, this took about a day.

Think about what the other Israelites must have been thinking, hearing Joshua command the sun and moon to stand still. That must have sounded like a bold command of faith. The boldness of Joshua affected the reality of all those around him.

Because of Joshua's faith, he commanded the sun to stand still, and it obeyed him! This was not a common request and was not within the realm of possibility for man. It could only be achieved by the LORD!

How bold is my faith in the situation or situations I face?

In Mark, Jesus stated, "*I assure you and most solemnly say to you, whoever says to this mountain, 'Be lifted up and thrown into the sea!' and does not doubt in his heart [in God's unlimited power], but believes that what he says is going to take place, it will be done for him [in accordance with God's will]'*" (Mark 11:23, AMP). When what comes out of our mouth lines up with God's will, and we don't doubt it in our heart, our mountains move!

Joshua's bold faith to command the sun and the moon to stand still, so the Israelites could see and win, lined up with God's will. Therefore, he knew that his enemies would be delivered into his hand.

Joshua believed this word from the LORD, even though it was starting to get dark, and it looked impossible! We are made in God's image, and when we speak, Creation obeys. We speak out of our heart, and we create our reality—good or bad!

Do I believe or doubt that what I am asking the LORD for in bold faith will manifest? Why?

_____

_____

_____

CHAPTER 7

FAITH THAT INFLUENCES

Matthew 9:18-26

The second healing recorded in this passage was of the daughter of the ruler. Jesus went to her house because her father had asked Him to. This dad had faith in God and had brought Jesus into the situation. In this way, he refused to accept his current reality as final.

Notice, the first thing Jesus did when He got to the ruler's house was send out the people who were saying, "She's dead." Why? Because they didn't have faith. Jesus knew they would influence the ones who did have faith.

WOW! That was a strong action. Jesus had to separate the ones who had doubt from the dad and daughter, so that the dad's faith could manifest. We may have very high faith, but what is our circle of influence like? Do others constantly tell us, "This is your reality," "That will never happen," or "Learn to live with it?" Maybe we should not talk to them about what we are believing for. Instead, bring people into the situation who will talk faith and life and not doubt. Ask the Holy Spirit "What is stopping my faith from manifesting?"

Who or what do I need to separate myself from that is causing me to doubt, pulling down my faith?

Joshua 14:6-15 and Deuteronomy 1:26-36

This is the story of Caleb, one of the twelve men Moses had sent out to spy out the Promised Land. At that time, he was only forty years old. Now, they were in the Promised Land, and Caleb, at the age of eighty-five, had gone to Joshua and asked him to give him his inheritance. It was an inheritance Caleb had faith he would one day receive, but he had waited forty-five years for this promise to manifest in his life.

Numbers 14:24 states, *"But my servant Caleb, because he had another spirit with him, and hath followed me fully, him will I bring into this land where into he went; and his seed shall possess it"* (KJV). Caleb received the promise because he *"fully"* followed God.

Does my lifestyle show me and others that I am wholeheartedly following God?

Caleb's lifestyle was what caused him and his seed to possess the promise! The promises written in the Scriptures apply to all of us. Some of us may have had prophetic words spoken over our life as well that we can stand on. When we think about the situation or the season of life we are in, what promise or promises come to mind?

142

When we think about our promise, and we try to keep our faith up, believing that what has been promised will come to pass, how is our lifestyle? Imagine being Caleb. He went in and saw the Promised Land, then returned to tell others all about it. Most of those around him saw it in a negative light, focusing on the impossibilities they would face. He was now in a situation where the LORD could do the impossible and show Himself strong on his behalf, and he wanted it.

Do I allow others to bring me down, causing me to lose my faith?

When it looks impossible or when a promise has been forgotten, do I give up? Or do I keep standing on the promise anyway?

Esther 4:1-17

In the time of Esther, she and her fellow Jews were fasting before she presented herself to the king. To give more background, Esther had been living with her uncle, Mordecai, when King Ahasuerus began a search for a new wife, and she was chosen to become his new queen. Haman, the king's right-hand man, didn't like the Jews and got the king to order that all Jews be killed. Hearing that Mordecai was by the gate wearing sackcloth, a sign of mourning, Esther went to speak with him and learned of Haman's plot. Mordecai asked Esther to go before the king and make a plea to save her people, the Jews. Esther was frightened by this prospect and sent word to her uncle expressing her fears. If she approached the king without being called, she risked being killed.

In this passage of Scripture, Esther asked Mordecai to have all the Jewish people fast and pray with her for three days. On the third day, she planned to approach the king, whether she lived or died.

This was a huge step of faith for Esther to take. Her uncle wanted her to approach the king, but she didn't want to act just because of who was asking her to do it. She wanted to hear from God. She would act AFTER she had fasted and prayed!

Esther was not impulsive. She was strategic and thought before she acted. This makes me think of something my pastor always says, "Being Spirit-led is NOT being brain-dead."

Applying Esther's actions to our own lives, we may need to step out in faith in a given situation. We may need to make a stand or stop tolerating and remaining silent in our current situation. Do we react impulsively, or do we pray first? Do we have someone in our life, like Mordecai, who can encourage us to embrace our calling and take bold steps of faith? We are at this point in our life right now, with certain people surrounding us for such a time as this!

Am I willing to take a bold step of faith? If so, what does this bold step of faith look like?

_____

_____

Have I prayed about this bold step of faith I am considering taking? Or do I react to what others are saying and just take a leap of faith?

Luke 5:17-26

Jesus was present and ready to heal when four men, who had a friend suffering with what was then called *"the palsy"* came bringing that friend to Him. They got the man there, only to realize that the house where Jesus was teaching was so full of people they couldn't get through the door. Undeterred, they decided to climb onto the roof, make a hole, and lower their friend down through the hole to Jesus. Think about the amount of effort involved and the work they went through to carry their friend with palsy to the place, then up onto that roof, and then lower him down to Jesus.

When the man was in front of Jesus, he was quickly healed, got up and walked out, carrying his bed. It was the faith and support of his friends, coupled with his own, that had made his healing possible.

Put yourself in that man's place. Maybe you need a financial miracle, a healing or just an encounter with the LORD to breathe new energy into your life. Do you have friends who will encourage you and keep building your faith? Do they make you feel as though anything is possible? Do they stop you from getting discouraged and help you redirect your focus back on Jesus?

Do they make their way to Jesus, or do they see a full house and stop?

What do those around me believe?

_____

_____

_____

What type of friends have I chosen
to encircle myself with?

_____

_____

_____

Maybe we are in the position of the friends, and we see someone at the edge of giving up. How do we respond? Do we bring them to Jesus, even if it's hard work? Do we bring them to the door, see that the house is full, and stop, or do we climb onto the roof, trying everything possible to get them to Jesus?

The faith of these friends was their belief. They believed that if their friend could get to Jesus, he would be healed. So, they supported him, doing what they needed to do to get their friend healed.

What do I believe?

_____

_____

_____

Does my faith get Jesus' attention?

_____

_____

_____

If my faith and belief affect those around me, am I affecting them positively or negatively? And why?

_____

_____

_____

Romans 14:1-23

The chapter starts with those weak in faith and continues to compare the food we eat with our faith level. Our faith is what we believe. We shouldn't boast of our faith in front of others, causing them to fall because they are unsure in some area. This chapter refers to everyone coming to Christ, and yet, at times, we try to force what we believe and see on others. We all have different standards that we uphold and live by. Some of our standards are held in our heart as convictions. It is wrong to push our convictions and faith on those around us who don't have the same level of conviction.

The Scriptures refer to people having different standards to live by. A person who teaches the Word of God is held to a higher standard of accountability than one who does not teach. It is, therefore, not right to force someone who is not teaching to live by the same standard as the one who _is_ teaching, just as it is wrong to cause someone to doubt their convictions and still act.

Do I push my faith and belief on others through speech or action? If so, why?

Verse 23 states, *"But the one who has misgivings feels miserable if he eats meat, because he doubts and doesn't eat in faith. For anything we do that doesn't spring from faith is, by definition, sinful"* (Romans 14:23, TPT). Comparing our faith, our convictions, and our liberty to others will lead us to act in doubt or compromise of what it is we should do. This is very bluntly called *sin* to us.

On the other hand, if we are strong in faith and cause others to doubt their beliefs and do according to what *we* feel they should do, then we have caused them to sin. We are not called to be the Holy Spirit to them. The LORD God is big enough to deal with others individually, just as He is ready to deal with us. He may be dealing with them in an area we are unaware of (because it is an inward area), while we think they should work on another area (maybe an outward area).

Am I a follower, doubting what and why I believe?

Do I bend my convictions, following others' leading? If so, why?

Romans 10:17

So then faith cometh by hearing, and hearing by the Word of God.

This scripture is pretty self-explanatory, showing us how to build our faith. According to Romans 12:3, we are all given a measure of faith. We can grow our faith or shrink our faith by what hear. We can either be optimistic or pessimistic. The choice is ours!

Let's use an example: Say that I am believing God for a raise, but my faith isn't really big enough to believe without doubting. Who am I surrounding myself with? If I surround myself with people who encourage me, speak the Scriptures and the character of God, my faith will begin to grow and deepen. I will eventually see what I am believing for come to pass. If I surround myself with people who are negative and live according to reality and what they see, then I may find myself losing hope, especially when the economy shows any negative sign.

We will become who we hang around with. Therefore, we are to surround ourselves with people who talk and believe the Scriptures. Hang out with people who discuss testimonies and what God is doing. Hang around people who have big faith and can dream, allowing them to rub off on you. Play music written according to the Scriptures. Listen to messages that talk about the area you are believing God for, and allow your faith to be stretched.

Is my faith growing or shrinking? And why?

_____

_____

_____

If it's shrinking, what can I do different this week to start growing my faith deeper?

_____

_____

_____

CHAPTER 8

APPLYING FAITH

2 Timothy 1:1-7

Paul started this letter speaking of Timothy's faith. The Passion Translation states verse 5 this way, *"As I think of your strong faith that was passed down through your family line. It began with your grandmother Lois, who passed it on to your dear mother, Eunice. And it's clear that you too are following in the footsteps of their godly example."* The Amplified Bible shows why this type of faith is so strong: *"I remember your sincere and unqualified faith [the surrendering of your entire self to God in Christ with confident trust in His power, wisdom and goodness, a faith] which first lived in [the heart of] your grandmother Lois and your mother Eunice, and I am confident that it is in you as well."*

I love how the Bible shows this as a generational faith, faith that was taught and then imitated. It was a strong faith in which they each surrendered their entire self to God in their heart and taught others to do the same.

According to Genesis 1, everything has seed in it. The grandmother, Lois, had yielded every part of her heart to God through Jesus. She didn't tell Jesus, "You can have this part of my heart, but you can't have this other part." She yielded her entire heart to God, and she spoke from her heart. So, as she was talking, nurturing and influencing those around her, she was indirectly teaching others to yield their heart, as she did. Her daughter was taught how to surrender her whole heart to God through Jesus and to be vulnerable to Him. In turn, her daughter, Eunice, taught her child, Timothy, how to yield his heart, the same as she had been taught by her mom.

We are all given a seed of faith. It's up to us to plant that seed and allow the Holy Spirit to grow and nurture it. Then, it's time to put our faith to work, time to teach others strong faith, time to purposely reproduce what is in us in those around us!

Do I have strong faith, as when my whole heart is surrendered to God through Jesus? If not, which part of my heart do I hold at a distance and still need to surrender?

_____

_____

_____

Am I mentoring others by encouraging and influencing them to surrender their whole heart to God through Jesus, building their faith, making it stronger today than it was yesterday?

_____

_____

_____

Which kind of belief (which is my faith) did I inherit and which kind of faith am I teaching? Are they the same or different? And why?

_____

_____
_____

_____

Challenge: Continue to study faith as you take the steps God aligns you with, as He starts to call you out of the boat of your comfort zone. Study in depth, with the help of the Holy Spirit, the additional scriptures you wrote on pages 26 and 34. Continue looking for more scriptures and allow the Holy Spirit to continually bring you further on your journey of faith.

It's time to step out of your comfort zone and encounter Jesus in a new and amazing way.

Author Contact Page

You may contact Crystal Callais by email at:

maintainingfreedom@yahoo.com

OTHER BOOKS BY CRYSTAL CALLAIS

There are times in our lives when we become stagnant and have a hard time breaking the repetitiveness that we have fallen into. This devotional was inspired to aid in bringing a fresh and deeper thought process into the study of God's Word. His will is that we continually have a fresh revelation of Him and see everything from His perspective, not our own. Crystal has included questions that will challenge you to think outside of your normal thought process or "out of the box." Allow every part of this devotional to be thought provoking, while positioning yourself to be vulnerable before God. If you do that, He will bring you into new depths in your relationship with Him, and you will find yourself *Going Deeper.*

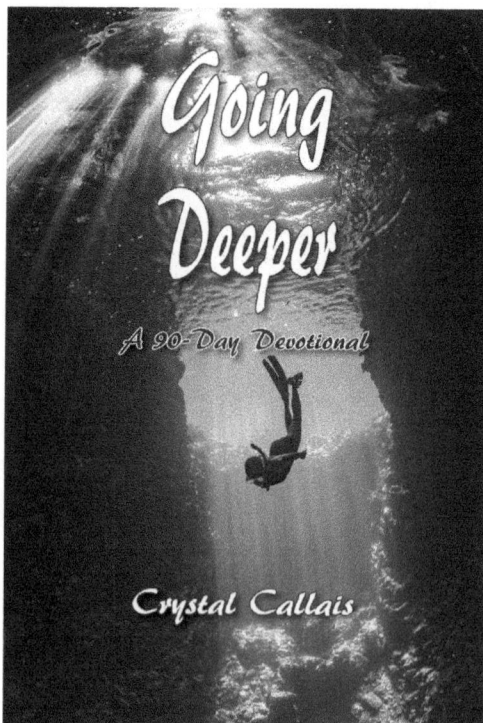

COMING SOON

Do you find yourself struggling with unanswered prayers and unanswered questions? With family unity? With fulfilling your call in God? With maintaining your peace, assurance, self-worth, or self-respect? Are you looking for a deeper, more intimate walk with Jesus Christ, your LORD and Savior? Join us as we journey from Genesis through Revelation, allowing the Holy Spirit to reveal to us a deeper understanding of who the LORD truly is; He is LOVE!

We will discuss patterns, mindsets and broken covenants that stand in our way, preventing us from fully experiencing what is ours. Our hope is that you will see how these mindsets, which are strongholds, pass from one generation to the next and how to stop them in their tracks and not allow them to continue down your family line.

Total freedom is possible for you! Through this course, you will learn how to maintain the freedom that was purchased at such a high price with the BLOOD of Jesus Christ on the cross of Calvary.

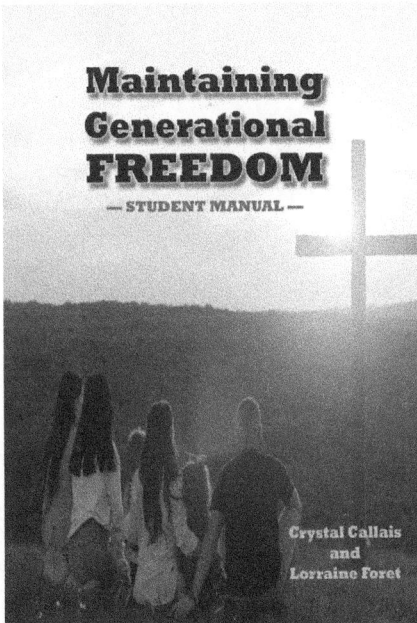

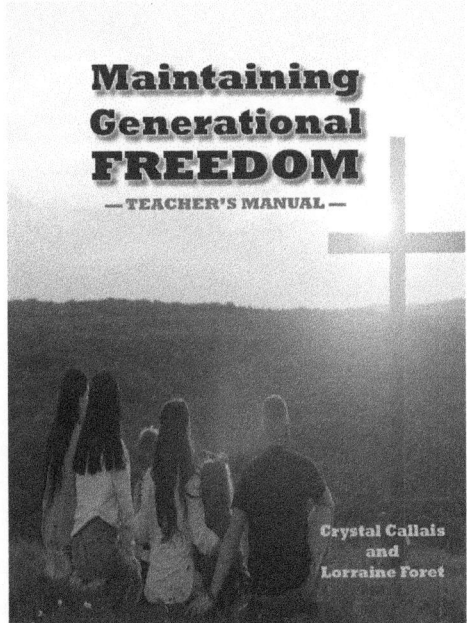

Maintaining Generational FREEDOM
— STUDENT MANUAL —

Crystal Callais
and
Lorraine Foret

Maintaining Generational FREEDOM
— TEACHER'S MANUAL —

Crystal Callais
and
Lorraine Foret

www.ingramcontent.com/pod-product-compliance
Lightning Source LLC
LaVergne TN
LVHW011332080426
835513LV00006B/301